RETURN
OF THE GOLD

RETURN
OF THE GOLD

The Journey of Jerry Colangelo and the Redeem Team

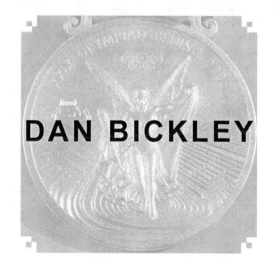

DAN BICKLEY

New York

Return of the Gold

The Journey of Jerry Colangelo and the Redeem Team

Cover Design by: 3 Dog Design
www.3dogdesign.net

ISBN 978-1-60037-637-5

Library of Congress Control Number: 2009927404

MORGAN · JAMES
THE ENTREPRENEURIAL PUBLISHER

Morgan James Publishing, LLC
1225 Franklin Ave., STE 325
Garden City, NY 11530-1693
Toll Free 800-485-4943
www.MorganJamesPublishing.com

Habitat for Humanity® Peninsula Building Partner

In an effort to support local communities, raise awareness and funds, Morgan James Publishing donates one percent of all book sales for the life of each book to Habitat for Humanity. Get involved today, visit **www.HelpHabitatForHumanity.org**.

THANK YOU

To Tami Bartlett Bickley, my editor and life partner ...

To Harvey Mackay, for an assist befitting Steve Nash ...

To Craig Miller, Sean Ford, and all the great people at USA Basketball ...

To every player, coach and source who gave their time and candor ...

To Skylar and Cameron, extremely smart children who understood why father was locked in his office for hours (so they could go to Disney World, of course) ...

To Jerry Colangelo, for the access and the latitude, showing why he's one of the best leaders in sports history ...

And to my longtime, lunchtime teammates back in the day. Namely, Tim, Jeff, Big E. and Joe Money, who'd punctuate the end of every victory by screaming the best word in the history of pickup basketball:

"Next!"

CONTENTS

PREFACE
The Game

....

Pick up a basketball. Clutch it with both hands. Bring it to your nose.

If it's an outdoor ball, you're sniffing an exhilarating blend of asphalt and rubber. If it's an indoor model, it's the musky aroma of crushed leather, a smell that can make you fall in love.

The scent immediately captured Jerry Colangelo, who bounced a basketball from a rough neighborhood called Hungry Hill all the way to the Naismith Memorial Basketball Hall of Fame. It instantly seduced Kobe Bryant, maybe the best talent the world has ever seen.

Long before a gold medal became their fellowship, these vastly different sportsmen – an Italian raised in America and an American raised in Italy – were bonded by a game, a ball, and that smell.

Bounce the ball in an empty gym. Listen to how it echoes off the walls and thumps against the polished floor. Go to the inner city, where heaven is a playground, and hear the chink of chain nets, the kind designed to catch, release and last all the way through icy winters. Listen closely. No sport has a better soundtrack than basketball, although it must be said that few things in life are more embarrassing the dull thud of an air ball. It's like jumping into a pool and missing the water.

When you're alone with that ball, you'll eventually wander to the free-throw line, where you can pretend the game is on the line. This is where the sport stops, where the sport seems welcoming, benign. It's the only time when no one can defend you, and the only time when the sport is about the individual.

It was on this line where Rumeal Robinson made two free throws with three seconds left in overtime, vaulting Michigan to a national championship in 1989.

It was on this line where Syracuse's Derrick Coleman missed the front end of one-and-one with 28 seconds left in the 1987 NCAA title game, allowing Indiana's Keith Smart the chance for a game-winning shot and a chunk of basketball immortality.

It was on that stripe where Skip Dillard – a Chicago playground product nicknamed "Money" because of his free-throw shooting prowess – missed the front end of a one-and-one opportunity in 1981, allowing underdog St. Joseph's to upset top-seeded DePaul and Mark Aguirre.

It was one of the greatest upsets in college basketball history, its impact felt all the way to the moment Dillard began robbing gas stations.

It was on that stripe in 1972 where a cold-blooded Olympian named Doug Collins shook off the pain and calmly beat the Russians. Or so we thought.

Finally, it was on that stripe where Michael Jordan once took flight, punctuating a memorable triumph in the 1987 slam-dunk contest. That dunk, among others, turned impressionable minds away from the fundamentals of team basketball, spawning a highlight-reel generation that believed they could leap all the way to NBA riches.

Now move back a few feet. This is three-point line. This is where the game gets difficult. This line changed the sport of basketball, enticing both the great shooters and those with little conscience.

In Game 1 of the 1992 NBA Finals, Jordan torched the Trail Blazers for six three-point shots in the first half, delivering his infamous shrug. Because of this line, few leads were ever safe. Because of this line, Robert Horry became known as Big Shot Bob.

It's a shot that requires strength, stamina and swagger. Before the inaugural three-point shooting contest at the 1986 NBA All-Star Game, Larry Bird walked into the locker room, eyeing the seven other competitors. He then asked who was playing for second place. That anecdote says as much about Bird as anything he's done on the court.

And beyond this line, Bryant and Dwyane Wade finally silenced the Spaniards, completing their mission and closing out one of the greatest games in Olympic history.

Along its winding, mercurial journey, there have been many variations of this beautiful game invented in Massachusetts back in 1891. There have been Showtime dynasties and blue-collar dynasties and gimmick teams that captured the imagination. There have been dramatic changes in style, uniform, footwear and athleticism.

But in the end, we have learned the hard way that basketball is the ultimate team endeavor. Only when you crack a defense with a series of deft passes does the game become magic. And as you run back down the court, you don't say a word or beat your chest or play to the cheering crowd. You find your man, play defense and remember what every coach has ever said:

Move your feet! Hands up! Box out!
Move the ball! Get back on defense! Teamwork!

That's the beauty of American basketball. And this is how it returned to our shores after an eight-year absence.

CHAPTER 1
Made in China

. . . .

Two buses roll past a makeshift security fence, past hundreds of Chinese basketball fans who have been waiting outside for hours.

Some carry cameras. Others just gawk. Earlier in the week, one zealot ran after the team bus in a rainstorm, screaming for Kobe Bryant.

Inside, Bryant shook his head, laughing at the absurdity of it all.

Tonight, the gathering is a bit antsy outside the InterContinental Beijing Financial Street Hotel. The sun is sinking away, and so are the 2008 Olympics. A sense of finality is in the air, an understanding that soon these giants will be gone, and with them, a little slice of history.

"They're here," a security man says into a tiny microphone.

The buses move past a second checkpoint, slowing to a crawl in front of the hotel lobby. A hatch on top of the second bus begins to move. A hand emerges, pushing the portal open.

Out pops the head of Carmelo Anthony. He works his torso free and gazes out at the crowd. He looks like a jack that just popped out of a box. A smile spreads on his face.

He grabs the medal around his neck, and holds it up for everyone to see.

It is gold: the medal, the moment and the grin. Housekeepers begin cheering. So do bellmen temporarily relieved of their posts. Normally reserved Chinese workers are literally jumping up and down, into one another's arms.

"I've never seen them act like this," said Raptors general manager Bryan Colangelo, looking out on the celebration. "They're normally so contained."

Less than two hours ago and only a few miles down the road, Team USA had reclaimed their heavyweight status, restoring a sense of global order in basketball. And they didn't have to wait long for their first victory parade.

It was the perfect ending to a near-perfect tournament.

Unlike the sour climate in Greece at the 2004 Olympics, where angry crowds hissed and whistled at anything involving Americans, and where wives of NBA players were verbally abused in the stands of basketball games, Team USA found their gold medals and a wonderful surprise in China.

Even before the Games began, they were no longer treated like ugly Americans. They were icons to worship. It was different. It was nice.

Much of the love was directed at Bryant, the Lakers superstar and the centerpiece of Nike's strategic invasion of China. It was also a reflection of the NBA's soaring popularity in this massive country, where LeBron James has his own museum and where basketball is fast becoming the sport of choice.

This massive cultural shift was on full display during the Beijing Olympics, where the past and the present seemed to clash on every corner. Middle-aged men and the old-timers still flock to table tennis parks, where they play pickup games of Ping-Pong and smoke cigarettes. Married couples with badminton racquets still swat about a birdie wherever there's an open patch of cement. And every morning, you'll find senior citizens practicing Tai Chi outdoors, in public parks, just to keep the blood flowing.

But the young kids?

They're wearing NBA gear and carrying basketballs. They are emulating a wide array of NBA players, wearing jerseys ranging from the obvious (Bryant, James) to the absurd (Steve Francis, Tim Hardaway). During the Olympics, a local newspaper ran a startling story stating that Yao Ming's jersey had actually dropped to No. 10 on the best-seller list in China.

Bryant was No.1, followed by Celtics star Kevin Garnett; the Rockets' Tracy McGrady; the Celtics' Paul Pierce; the Nuggets' Allen Iverson; the Wizards' Gilbert Arenas; James; the Heat's Dwyane Wade; and Magic center Dwight Howard.

Good thing Chairman Mao wasn't around to hear that.

It's a remarkable change in allegiance. In China, Yao Ming will always be a beloved figure, a pioneer, a humanitarian and a goodwill ambassador. But on the court, Yao is like a brontosaur. His lumbering game doesn't exactly captivate the imagination of the locals anymore, and now his jersey sales are plummeting.

These days, the Chinese are into basketball for the aerial thrills and the exhilaration, for proof that man really can fly. It's not just the national pride that once came with exporting an NBA player that's behind this renaissance.

Like all sports fans, the Chinese want something new and exciting. Mostly, they want Kobe. So sorry.

"I don't know when this all happened," Bryant said. "I was here in the summer of 2007, and it wasn't like this. Something just exploded. I guess we should all thank Yao (Ming). He's the one who built the bridge."

Indeed, hoop dreams are everywhere in China, and they can be found deep in the craw of communism. Travel to Tiananmen Square, where stone-faced soldiers march in unison, reminding you who's in charge. Pass under the famous mural of Chairman Mao. Just before the entrance to the Forbidden City, you won't believe your eyes.

Outside the main gate where dynasties lived and emperors roamed, there is a regulation-sized basketball court. It has dirty, frayed nets. The playing surface is green field turf with painted lines. It feels like Rucker Park dropped in the middle of Beijing. It lends a bizarre feel to these historical, sacred grounds.

In some ways, the exporting of basketball to faraway lands is no different than some of the other strange changes in Beijing. A gleaming new Cadillac dealership is housed next to a freeway jammed with homogenous, compact cars. For a country weaned on tea, Starbucks has also become strangely popular. Meanwhile, Coca-Cola and McDonald's are staples of daily life.

As this emerging country opens its doors wider and wider to the ways and businesses of the West, more than 1.3 billion consumers wait inside. As a result, China was not only the host country for the 2008 Olympics. It represented the last, great untapped market. And the NBA, like every other corporation, wanted a bigger, stronger market share.

As a result, no one in power wanted to criticize the host's country for anything, even when circumstances called for outrage. The International Olympic Committee didn't seem too eager to investigate China's baby-faced gymnasts. The organization didn't dare scold the host country for blocking Web sites and censoring journalists. Meanwhile, the United States Olympic Committee didn't seem too interested in defending the cause of former Olympian and Darfur advocate Joey Cheek, who had his visa revoked a day before leaving for China.

And everyone just gulped and turned away when news broke of two elderly Chinese women, ages 77 and 79, being sent away to a re-education camp for *desiring* to protest.

With their reputation already damaged abroad, members of Team USA knew the importance of good manners at the 2008 Olympics. But at times, their approach felt like kowtowing, and it made for some uncomfortable questions for players who chose not to criticize

China's human rights record. After all, Bryant once taped a public service announcement on the subject, and James once promised to rally his team around the plight in Darfur.

It led many to believe in a conspiracy of silence, that the NBA was effectively muzzling its superstars.

That wasn't exactly true. During the buildup to the Olympics, NBA players were simply shown the financial benefit of silence, of playing the game on and off the court. One instance of this occurred near the end of training camp in Las Vegas, when NBA Deputy Commissioner Adam Silver delivered a special presentation to Team USA.

Silver reminded the players that Nike had 6,000 stores in China. The company had also sponsored the opening of James' museum in Shanghai. And it went without saying that 11 of 12 players in the room were Nike clients. Of the group, only Dwight Howard failed to draw a check from the shoe giant. Howard had signed with Adidas.

Silver also pointed out that there's more Internet traffic on NBA.com coming from China than there is from the United States, which is a technicality given China's huge population advantage, but a truth just the same.

And then came the clincher, the story of how actress Sharon Stone sabotaged her own marketability in China with one loose comment on the red carpet. It was the infamously stupid sound byte that occurred after the tragic earthquake in the Sichuan Province, which swallowed schoolchildren and left millions homeless:

"Well, you know, it was very interesting because at first I'm not happy with the way the Chinese are treating the Tibetans because I don't think anyone should be unkind to anyone else ... and so I have been very concerned about how to think and what to do about that because I don't like that. And then, I've been concerned with how we should deal with the Olympics because they're not being nice to the Dalai Lama, who's a good friend of mine. And then all this earthquake and all this stuff happened, and I thought, 'Is that karma, when you're not nice, that the bad things happen to you?' "

Silver pointed out how Stone was promptly banned in China, and how Christian Dior was forced to pull her off all its advertisements.

"She lost a $25 million deal based on that statement," Silver said.

The players snapped to attention. "Oohs" and "ahhs" were heard inside the room, and they immediately understood Silver's message. Just like that, Team USA morphed into an apolitical brotherhood with little time for humanitarian missions. James soon declared that sports and politics just don't mix, and that the collective focus was 100 percent basketball. Don't think these guys don't know their business.

Still, the emphasis on image was best symbolized by their head coach, Mike Krzyzewski, who had his own financial interests in mind. During the final mini-camp in Las Vegas, Krzyzewski helped close, and celebrate a new $40 million partnership between Nike and Duke University. There were investments to protect, investments to grow, and after each

Olympic triumph, Krzyzewski began every press conference with gushy tributes for the opponent.

"I think in some respects over the years, we've been pretty arrogant," Krzyzewski said before the team left for Beijing. "It's not our game. It's the world's game."

Legend has it that NBA Commissioner David Stern once traveled to China hoping to spark the fires of globalization. The customs agent looked at his passport and declared, "Ahh, red oxen!" That was back when Michael Jordan's Bulls ruled the world, emerging as a global phenomenon.

Now, 10 years after Jordan's last championship, the NBA has grown deep roots in this country where some 300 million people play basketball. For reference, that's roughly the population of the United States.

But economics were only half the story, and there were far more noble reasons for the American team to exhibit impeccable manners.

At root was the high-minded mission implemented by Jerry Colangelo, who took over the reigns of Team USA in 2005 and reformed the entire operation. He made it clear to his team that he wanted to change the image and perception of American basketball players, and it started with big helpings of humility and grace. He looked each of his players in the eyes when making his case, to be sure there were no misunderstandings.

The players listened, and they responded.

They worked at appearing dignified. They placed their hands over their hearts during the national anthem and resisting the urge to bark at referees during the game. They kept the swagger and gratuitous dancing to a minimum. As a group, they had never looked better.

Finally, whatever issues any of these players had with a communist government quickly faded away once they encountered the Chinese people, who were unfailingly polite, gentle and kind to most all of their foreign visitors.

Hotel security was at a level that would befit world leaders, not a basketball team. During a pre-Olympic exhibition in Shanghai, traffic was literally shut down so Team USA could travel without incident, and the level of coordination stunned Jim Boeheim, legendary Syracuse coach and Team USA assistant.

"We went 50 miles an hour right through the city," Boeheim said. "Not on a highway, either. This was right through the city. Then you'd get on a highway and all the entrances were blocked. It was impressive, maybe the best I've ever seen. You try to do that in New York, and there would be a few guys with guns getting out of their cars."

When Team USA finally took the court in Beijing, they were treated to rousing ovations. Chinese fans went bonkers when any of the American players dunked during warmups, as if they were witnessing a rare and spectacular circus.

In 1992, the rest of the world fawned over the Dream Team. On a smaller scale, that's just what it felt like among the locals in Beijing, and the scene outside the team hotel was just a small slice of the adulation heaped on the American team.

Colangelo, the team's architect and mastermind, looked like a proud father, holding a bouquet of flowers and appearing flush with relief. Wade carried an unlit victory cigar in his mouth. There were hugs all around, deep and meaningful, and one by one, the players disappeared into lobby elevators.

Later that night, they filtered down to the unofficial team dinner, and the giant conference room was electric with triumph. Bryant embraced Krzyzewski, and moved to a table with his own family. He bounced his young daughter on his lap. Later that night, Bryant broke from the team, departing on his own flight home.

The gold-medal game against Spain was a delicious end to a long journey. It represented the first major victory against international competition in eight years. It was an exquisite game that seemed to punctuate everything the Americans hoped to accomplish, from teamwork to cohesion to poise under pressure.

It was a game worthy of a Redeem Team, a game that seemed to transcend the sport. And for the first time in a long time, not an ill word could be spoken about the U.S. Olympic basketball contingent.

"It was like Villanova-Georgetown," Krzyzewski said. "But this time, Georgetown won."

As the victory party raged on, Doug Collins posed for pictures with a gold medal around his neck, the one he never received in Munich, Germany. Stern showed up looking tired but satisfied, and someone whispered that he'd been out closing even more business deals over the weekend. Near the end of the party, Collins and the older Colangelo clasped hands.

"You know what you've done?" Collins said to Colangelo. "You've set the bar. Now, that team in 2012 knows exactly what's expected of them. You've changed the entire culture of USA Basketball."

And maybe the culture of basketball in the USA.

The next morning, there was one last scene to behold. It was 5:15 a.m., exactly one hour before the official caravan was to leave for the airport. The lobby was empty, and darkness seemed to suffocate all sound. This is when James, Anthony and Wade walked into the hotel from their own private victory party, without security detail or posses.

They moved through the lobby like lions back from a nocturnal hunt. Each wore the glow of victory.

Many have shared in this triumph. From top down, many deserve credit. For those who had given an arduous three-year commitment to the cause, the sense of accomplishment was profound. But only three players know what it's like to be branded as the future of American basketball, only to get stuck with that bronze medal and scarlet letter from the 2004 Olympics in Athens.

They are James, Wade and Anthony, and on the ground floor of redemption, this is their triumph. It hardly matters that they have less than an hour to shower, pack and get back down to the lobby.

And now that the sun has emerged, the only one with a problem is Deron Williams, the talented young point guard for the Utah Jazz.

Williams has done the unthinkable. He forgot to check his luggage the night before, as required, and is now carrying a bulging suitcase through customs. He is tired, and wearing dark sunglasses inside. His body starts to slump realizing, he might have to get in another line and check the bag, or tell someone else to do it for him.

A USA Basketball official senses the tension, and quickly comes to the rescue. He tells Williams not to worry. He rubs Williams on the back for good measure, to let him know that everything is OK.

After some of the previous messes left behind by Team USA, this was nothing.

CHAPTER 2
The Big Penny

· ·

The Big Penny changed American basketball.

If you're not familiar with the term, then you missed the lowest point of Carmelo Anthony's public life.

In the Baltimore ghetto, the Big Penny is street slang for the bronze medal. The phrase showed up on a DVD called, "*Stop Snitching*," an underground production that placed a giggling Anthony in the company of an alleged drug dealer talking street-corner smack.

Like what happens to those who become police informants.

Or mocking the street value of that bronze medal Anthony recently brought home from Greece.

Narrator: "Ask him what he did with his penny?"

Background voice: "Who?"

Narrator: "What he did with his bronze medal they gave him?"

Background voice, to Anthony: "Why you ain't wearing it, yo?"

Narrator: "He just told me he threw the (medal) overseas."

Anthony: "It's in a lake somewhere."

Narrator: "He says, 'I wasted my whole summer chasing a big penny."

Background voice: "A big penny?"

Anthony: "It's as big as (expletive), like this (making a circle with his hands)."

Narrator: "How the hell is he gonna tell a bitch he's worth 100 mill and he chased a big penny for two months straight?"

Before the cameo appearance drew mainstream attention later that year, there would be even more trouble for Anthony. Airport security found marijuana in his backpack as he tried to board a team plane. (A friend swore the drugs were his, and charges were dropped). Then came a scuffle in a New York City nightclub.

If the 2004 Olympic team represented the worst of American basketball, then Anthony was the poster child of that team, a player who got benched, complained about playing time and generally resembled the worst the NBA had to offer.

Like many of his generation, Anthony was young, raw and remarkably gifted. He was silky, smooth, and could score almost effortlessly. He was the high school rival of LeBron James. As a freshman in college, he led Syracuse to a national championship, averaging 22.2 points and 10 rebounds per game.

And then he was gone, off to the NBA.

"Those are very difficult numbers to reach in college," Boeheim said. "Then to win a national championship as a freshman and be the main guy on the team - *the main guy on the team* - nobody has ever done that.

"So his one year has a lot of firsts, a lot of things. The thing I always remember about him was he was one of the guys. He never acted like a one-and-done player. That's the real danger, when a guy acts like a one-and-done player, which is what happens today. He never acted like that. As the season broke out, you might've had a feeling he was going to go (turn professional), but he never acted that way right through the national championship game. And that was an important part of us being able to be successful because he never brought any of that into the equation."

A few months later, James jumped to the NBA as well. He signed a $90 million deal with Nike straight out of high school, before playing a minute with the Cavaliers. He would be the first overall selection in the 2003 Draft, while Anthony would be selected at No. 3.

Wade, meanwhile, took the conventional approach, the old-school route to riches.

In his third year at Marquette University, Wade became a national sensation. The NCAA Tournament was his coming-out party, and Wade carried his team to the Final Four just as Larry Bird had done with Indiana State many years ago. Along the way, Wade laid a sensational triple-double (29 points, 11 rebounds, 11 assists) on top-ranked, top-seeded Kentucky. He would be drafted fifth, the highest slot ever for a player from Marquette.

Together, these three players symbolized the future of the NBA. When Anthony and James met for the first time on an NBA court, it was a colossal event, packaged as the beginning of the next great individual rivalry. Celebrities, media and more than 20,000 fans jammed into the Gund Arena in Cleveland.

That game wasn't worth the hype, but soon, James and Wade proved better than advertised. James was freakishly athletic for his size and an instant impact player, while Wade led the Heat to a championship in his second season, carrying Shaquille O'Neal along for the ride.

But Anthony veered left. Like many NBA players, he came from a hardscrabble background, from the rough streets of Baltimore. And while he seemed pleasant enough, he carried a certain street swagger. His body was covered with tattoos. He wore his hair in corn-rows held firm by bandanas or headbands, and often accompanied by a cocked baseball cap.

When the incident sheet began to grow, Anthony was easily typecast as the classic new-wave NBA thug. He represented a window into a league that always seems to be fighting perception problems and cultural divides.

"When you look at it, there have been three or four (incidents) with Carmelo," Boeheim said. "But, really, if you separate them, they're really relatively small. But sometimes, what happens is, when you do have something, the article or story compiles the history, so it looks worse than I think it really is. But, you know, he's young, and a couple of his friends got him in trouble a couple of times and he's got himself in trouble a couple of times. You learn from those experiences. That's all you can do.

"You have to look at what kind of person he is. Not only has he given money to us and (the city of) Baltimore, but he's gone back and held events for kids, he's done stuff in Denver, Baltimore and Syracuse already ... I think you have to look at the total picture when you look at anybody. And when you look at his total picture, he's done a lot of good things."

So why was the message getting lost? How did our country begin to dislike its own game and its own players with such a passion?

In Olympic basketball, it's easy to plot the downward arc. A tournament is held every four years, and from 1936-2000, the United States won 12 of 14 gold medals. But cracks in the foundation began to develop. After barely prevailing in 2000, Team USA became a national embarrassment four years later. The country that had invented the sport was shamed into reform.

In the NBA, the gradual erosion of image and popularity was slow and inevitable, triggered by many factors. Waves of young players joined the league straight out of high school or after a short stint in college, thus lowering the talent level and collective maturity of the league. The hip-hop culture created a disconnect with some parts of the audience, a culture whose music stresses street life, violence, handguns and self-glorification. And while this new breed of freakishly gifted athletes amazed audiences with their athleticism, they often seem to appall with their lack of fundamental skill.

The NBA has long discounted the impact of this perception problem. Yet it's the NBA that instituted a dress code for its players, prohibiting things like baggy pants and cocked hats. It's the NBA that raised its minimum age to 19. And it's the NBA that once air-brushed Allen Iverson on the cover of a league publication, removing all tattoos from the front of his arms.

Translation: It's a problem.

"People have to realize that at this point in time, the NBA is full of a lot of young guys, and a lot of people don't like the hip-hop culture," said Raptors star Chris Bosh. "The league is going to be a reflection of its total makeup. And a lot of guys came straight out of high school, so the league is still very young right now. That's the perception of everything. People who might not necessarily like the hip-hop culture wouldn't like the makeup of the league.

"But that's our culture. The hair, some people expressing themselves through tattoos, different types of clothing and everything ... that's what we do. That's what we're used to, and sometimes people don't understand that. I think if they just would take the time to understand where we're coming from and what we like and the differences we all have, I think we can all get along better. If a guy has tattoos, it doesn't mean he's a bad, mean person. I know the nicest dudes who are tatted from head to toe. It's just a matter of not understanding. In some cases, it could be discriminatory. But that's part of life. And what people don't understand often is what makes people afraid."

Besides, self-expression had nothing to do with the problem. The real problem was the quality of basketball, the individuality that had permeated basketball, and what it represents.

In the 21st century, great players are no longer the handiwork of iconic coaches, great systems and great seasoning. Most elite players will star for their high school teams, bounce through one year of college with the least resistance possible, and then get on an NBA payroll.

It makes economic sense. In the NBA, the average annual salary entering the 2008-09 season was $4.65 million. Most important, a player must work his way through a four-year rookie contract before becoming eligible for the lucrative maximum deal. If you desire NBA riches, you have to get the clock ticking as soon as possible.

Along the way, these elite players find many distractions. They usually funnel through the Amateur Athletic Union, which stages basketball tournaments for all ages, all over the country. These tournaments expose star talent to scouts, college coaches, street agents, sponsors, and other star talent. It is here were reputations are made and broken. And for many inside the loop, it's a big part of the problem.

Portland Trail Blazers coach Nate McMillan watched his son, Jamelle, work his way through the current system, eventually signing a scholarship with Arizona State. And he couldn't believe how much the game had changed.

"When I was growing up, you went from town to town," McMillan said. "Now, you're going from city to city. My son saw the United States before he was 17. He played in Virginia.

He played in Florida. He played in California. He played in Texas. He played in all of these places and he wasn't even in high school.

"It was just amazing that AAU had become so large, and so much money had been invested. But that style of basketball ..."

McMillan paused for five full seconds.

"On some teams, the coaches really do try to teach the game," he said. "But it is more of a showcase for a few individuals more than teaching the team game. We went from taking experienced college players, seniors and juniors, to where we were taking high school players and bringing them into the NBA. Well, what type of potential do they show for you to take them at such a young age? They show the ability to score. And that's what they become. And everybody tries to do that.

"They haven't shown that they can lead a team. They haven't shown the basics of knowing how to play the game, and we're jumping all over them at such a young age. A lot has suffered from that sense. College basketball, you have maybe a few universities that are very talented. And the NBA is only now starting to get its sex appeal back because, for a while, we were young and our stars were very young. And the league is much younger than it was years ago.

"For me, as an NBA coach, I know I have to almost approach my team as a college coach does. You have to teach them. So we spend a lot of time on the basics, on learning the game, because our athletes, they come here and they haven't been taught. Most of these guys are high school stars who scored. They averaged 30 or 40 points a game. But they've never been in a defensive stance because they've never had to play defense. They don't know anything about ball movement because they've always had the ball."

Catering to individual talent is a fundamental issue in American basketball, tearing at the fabric of the game. A promising player will likely be pampered and placed on a pedestal. The great ones end up with ESPN cameras in their gymnasiums before attending their senior proms. Vanity takes over. They learn to take what is so readily given.

A month before the Summer Games began, Collins came to Las Vegas to speak to the 2008 Olympic team During his visit, he went to an AAU tournament. He found a star 14-year- old giving interviews and referring to himself in the third person. He watched a coach get kicked out of the game, and then invite the referee to meet him in the parking lot when it was over.

It would take great parenting and great perspective for a young athlete not to be affected by all the fawning and corruption inside this gravy train culture.

"It's just so out of balance," Collins said. "We're flying these kids all over the country, setting them up in hotels. They're playing basketball and then speaking to reporters. We're ranking these kids when they're 14. We want to know who is the top eighth-grader in the country. You know how many times I played on television before I went to the NBA? Once.

"I don't want to do that old school-new school stuff, but that's not what this is about. This is about what we're pumping into these kids, who then go and become NBA players. When is the last time they've ever been told, 'No?' When was the last time they've been told they have to earn their playing time? When was the last time they've been coached, really coached, and had demands of excellence placed on them?

"You can't do it when they're in high school because you're afraid they're going to transfer. If they're on your AAU team and they don't like you or don't get to play, they're going to another AAU team. A lot of these college coaches become very territorial, and you're walking on egg shells with these kids. I feel bad because I look back on where I got to be, and every level I played at, I think about the coaches who put demands of excellence on me, what that did for me, and where I'd be without that training.

"I feel badly for these young kids. I really do. It's not their fault. It's what we've created."

The NBA also contributed heavily to the problem. After centralizing its marketing efforts and making a fortune off of Michael Jordan, the league's desire to showcase individual stars began to backfire.

"Guys are trying to entertain too much," said Mannie Jackson, former Mr. Basketball in Illinois and current owner of the Harlem Globetrotters. "I really believe David Stern has done a miraculous job, the way he turned it around and built value into the league. But there's always garbage when you do that. There's always a byproduct you don't want. And part of that byproduct is the embracing and the romance of entertainment and exhibition.

"When we play the Washington Generals, they allow us to do what we do. But I can't put the same team on the floor against Michigan State or Syracuse. They won't comply. I watch the NBA, these guys are the greatest athletes in the world, and they're letting players get away with that kind of stuff. They're complying.

"It's the fancy cross-over dribbles, the bad fundamentals, and guys trying to dunk every shot. We think it's great basketball. We think it's entertaining. But then you put them against a team from Lithuania that knows nothing of that convention and doesn't care. You see how our guys struggle, and you think, 'These are the players we're paying millions of dollars a year?'

"I grew up in a small town in the southern part of Illinois, in a suburban town. There were about 25 black families in the town, and maybe 10 of us in the high school. We had an Italian coach, a disciplinarian. We went to play kids in Chicago. It was the urban kids playing the suburban kids.

We had the discipline. We played with structure. We knew how to run in lanes, and how to cut at the right angles. We sat on the bench if we dunked. But we always won against that stuff."

As the game became a celebration of the individual, elite players in America rarely needed to become grounded, well-rounded team players. As Collins pointed out, most of them are talented enough to outrun their mistakes, and do so many times during the course of every game. But inevitably, the NBA became more athletic, and less skilled.

It became more exciting and more infuriating all at the same time.

"People always say, 'Tell me something about Michael Jordan,'" Collins said. "I'll tell you about Michael Jordan. You look at him, you see incredible skill, speed, quickness, all those things. You see his genius mind. What people forgot to realize is he was the most fundamentally solid player in the game, from the footwork to the attention to detail to busting his ass every single day. That's what got lost with Michael Jordan."

Fortunately, the Olympics have always provided moments of clarity for American basketball. The 2000 Olympics in Sydney produced one of the best made-for-television moments in basketball history, the moment when Vince Carter literally jumped over a 7-foot-2 French player and dunked the basketball.

The French media tagged the play with a great phrase, calling it "le dunk de la mort." The dunk of death. Yet in that same tournament, it was becoming clear that something was wrong with the highlight-reel culture. The world was catching up fast to America's brand of basketball. Lithuania came dangerously close to pulling off an upset in the semifinals, and France was actually an obstacle in the championship game.

Four years later, the entire system crashed in Athens.

There are many reasons why the 2004 Olympic basketball team will forever own a special place in history. They lost three times, becoming the first team of professionals not to win a gold medal. They were blown out by Puerto Rico.

There was a nasty rift between the team's coach, Larry Brown, and the hierarchy of USA Basketball. After arriving in Greece woefully under-prepared, Brown verbally distanced himself from the team at every possible moment, placing blame on the team's selection committee, his roster and the lack of preparation time.

Brown did little coaching, and his lineups were bizarre. He stuck with Allen Iverson, Stephon Marbury and Richard Jefferson, largely ignoring James, Wade, Anthony and Amaré Stoudemire. Team morale soon crumbled.

During a semifinal win over Spain, Brown called a late, unnecessary timeout with the game already in hand. This infuriated Spain's coach Mario Pesquera, and the two men were involved in a post-game screaming match, during which Brown was overheard saying, "Do you want some of me?"

Oh, did he ever. And so did the rest of the world.

"I had, I stress *had* respect for Larry Brown," Pesquera huffed in the post-game press conference.

By tip-off of the Olympic semifinals two nights later, the anti-America sentiment in Greece was noxious and thick. The environment and their opponent - Manu Ginobili and his gritty band of Argentinian brothers - were too much to handle. The Americans lost again, and their gold-medal chase was over.

There were many systemic, predictable reasons for the meltdown in Greece. But this team seemed to symbolize something much worse than a third-place finish.

The American players were exposed by strong, smart cohesive teams with no egos and few weak links. They were easily confused, rattled, coaxed into bad shots and one-on-one battles. When in trouble, they did what all NBA stars do: They flung themselves toward the basket and waited for a foul call and the star treatment that never arrived.

The skilled players had trumped the world's best athletes, proving that basketball was the ultimate team game. It was *"Hoosiers"* in reverse, and many of our players in Athens conveniently fit the new

NBA archetype, the kind that was making many fans long for the good old days.

Fair or not, Anthony seemed to be the prime offender. He placed a towel over his head during the loss to Argentina. After games, he disrobed as he walked off the court, showing off his ink-stained body. It was a powerful metaphor for all that seemed to ail the NBA, and suddenly, the results backed up the perception problem.

"If we were able to send our best guys over there every time since 1992, we would've won," said Charles Grantham, former executive director of the NBA Players Association. "The coaching and the politics of those teams we put together, all of those things became a factor in how we performed and how we looked.

"The thing that bothered me is that some of the things coming back had racial overtones. Or a guy wasn't showing his patriotism. Look, I'm a players' guy, and our guys take their lead from leadership. Tell them what they have to do. I think, clearly, there was not an understanding of what our role was. And that brings you back to the selection process."

Whatever the reasons, the bottom line screamed for help. In two successive major international tournaments - the 2002 World Championship and the 2004 Olympics - Team USA had lost six times combined, badly tarnishing the image of an American game. In some horrific twist of irony, the player who best symbolized the individualization of American basketball - Stephon Marbury - pocketed the Olympic single-game scoring record (31 points), which he owns to this day.

Alas, they all came home with a Big Penny, a sour stigma and a country that wanted no part of Team USA.

"We had people from our country booing us," said Jazz forward Carlos Boozer, also an Olympian in 2004. "In a sense of words and what was being said about us, people were booing us. It was tough to take the criticism, especially when the young guys didn't even play that much."

Something had to be done.

Luckily, the right someone needed a new job.

CHAPTER 3
Pick Me Up

∙ ∙

Before the phone rang, Jerry Colangelo was adrift. Itchy. Men who build empires can not sit around and solve crossword puzzles.

He was in the process of losing his office at US Airways Center, the one with a great balcony and scenic view of downtown Phoenix, the city he helped create and define. He no longer had a significant role in the Suns, having cashed in his hand with the sale to brash new owner, Robert Sarver.

His son, Bryan, was no longer working maniac hours just down the hall, eager to bring dad that missing championship. Bryan was now the general manager in another country, landing in Toronto after Sarver cleared the decks and the Colangelo influence in Phoenix.

At age 65, Colangelo had his trophies and memories and every reason to enjoy a full retirement. He was globally respected, and flush with money. He even had a World Series championship, and a loving wife who consistently kicks his tail at Scrabble.

But there was a void. His beloved basketball franchise was no longer under his control, no longer a family affair. And truth is, baseball was never that good to Colangelo, at least not until that memorable World Series against the Yankees.

He once played the game. He was a promising young pitcher at Bloom High School on the South Side of Chicago, the ace of a staff that also included future Major League pitcher Jim Bouton. Then Colangelo hit the wall.

Actually, it was home plate.

"It's the consolation game of a national American Legion tournament in 1957," Colangelo said. "We're down to our last batter, and I'm it. I get hit with a pitched ball on my left hand, and the umpire called a foul ball. I was so mad, I went down and punched the ground . I broke every bone in my hand."

It was the day Colangelo lost any future in Major League Baseball.

"I came back and pitched at the University of Illinois," he said. "But when my cast came off, I couldn't throw hard anymore. I was more of a junk thrower. I became a relief pitcher."

Four decades later, Colangelo joined the ranks of Major League Baseball, and quickly rankled his fellow owners. He spent wildly to propel ticket sales inside a dispassionate Phoenix market, hoping to reverse a 25-percent loss in ticket sales from the inaugural season. He awarded huge deals to Jay Bell, Matt Williams, Todd Stottlemyre and many others. He won an arbitration hearing against catcher Jorge Fabregas in the amount of $875.000, and in a stunning move, he ripped up the favorable ruling, handing Fabregas a two-year deal worth $2.9 million.

In his experience, such shows of generosity had always paid off handsomely in the NBA, creating a strong culture of loyalty and a destination point for potential free agents. It made athletes want to play for him, and his track record with the Suns was beyond reproach.

In Major League Baseball, it bought Colangelo instant results, a contending team and a lot of new enemies. It alienated the old-boy network running the sport, competitors who didn't like Colangelo's lack of financial restraint, or how he inflated the salary structure. Many believe it was this resentment inside league offices that kept the All-Star Game from coming to Phoenix, normally a standard reward in cities that build new stadiums with public money.

"Although I thought I had some people in my corner, like (George) Steinbrenner and Jerry Reinsdorf, many of the others thought I was a basketball guy coming into their game," Colangelo said. "I understood. I respected it. It was OK. I didn't speak any trash, I didn't lay down any ultimatums. We just went about our business, and I don't think there were any issues at all in the first year. We went to meetings. We took our lumps.

"But I think our success did have a negative impact on people toward us, and me. Because we had too much success too fast. We won three divisional titles and a World Series, and you're not supposed to do that. I think that led to an attitude where it was real easy to throw me over the side."

It was petty and stupid. During the first five years of existence, the Diamondbacks won three division titles and a World Series. The seven-game triumph over the Yankees in 2001 was considered among the best World Series in history, with the Diamondbacks rallying in the last inning of the season against famed closer Mariano Rivera. And when a bloop single from Luis Gonzalez kissed the outfield grass, Colangelo had delivered Arizona's first major professional championship.

Yet the debt was real and mounting, and Colangelo needed help. Once, at a function, he ran into Arte Moreno, a friend and a local businessman who made a fortune in billboards.

"Why don't you sell me the team?" Moreno said.

"Write me a check," Colangelo countered.

The two men smiled. Moreno wanted a hometown discount. Colangelo couldn't sell his partners short. The moment passed, a moment that was only half-serious to begin with. Moreno ended up buying the Angels, writing a check for $180 million. Colangelo raised capital by bringing in more investors, who eventually staged a hostile takeover.

The situation was getting sticky, especially for a man accustomed to making all the decisions.

For instance, while forming his baseball team in the mid-1990s, he had newspaper readers submit a list of potential names for the franchise.

The list was then pared down to two, and then Colangelo passed out votes to key members of the organization. It was a classic case of getting everyone involved, spreading the power, distributing ownership among his people.

Except in the final secret ballot, the Scorpions beat the Diamondbacks handily. And on the spot, Colangelo exercised his veto power. Democracy be damned. His franchise was not going to be named after an arthropod.

But the debt Colangelo incurred while running the Diamondbacks lessened his power, and ultimately led to a philosophical clash and nasty divorce with the organization. And the new regime running the Diamondbacks was quick to erase the Colangelo brand, changing the team colors and logo almost overnight.

While the parties have since reconciled, it was a long time before Colangelo could step foot into a stadium to watch a team he brought to Arizona. For years, Major League Baseball executives went out of their way to applaud the fiscal control exercised by the Diamondbacks new regime, a group that was run by Ken Kendrick and Jeff Moorad

It is a slap in the face to a man whose only motive was winning, to a man who orchestrated the best start any expansion franchise has ever enjoyed.

"All I can tell you is, I'd do it all over again, and I'd do it the same way," Colangelo said. "I will never apologize regarding anything that was done with the baseball franchise. I wasn't doing anything that was off the wall. Everything was done with a lot of thought, gut-wrenching decisions, and buy-in from all the partners. They knew we'd have a very rough time rebuilding while we paid off the debt. Everyone went in with their eyes wide open.

"When Ken (Kendrick) and I really got into it was over the selection of Stephen Drew with the first pick. He thought it was crazy and dumb because (hard-line agent) Scott Boras represented him, and we'd never be able to sign him. I told him that our baseball people thought it was worth a shot. We had a knockdown, drag-out (fight) on that one. That was the beginning of the parting of the ways.

"But let me say this: In all my years of being in sports and knowing owners in all kinds of sports, I know that owners come in different shapes, sizes, pocketbooks, the whole thing. But I've never found a fan base out there leading the cheers for a franchise that is fiscally running a good ship. Because most of the fans couldn't care less. All they want to do is win. And so, some of the more popular owners in sports are the ones willing to go to the wall and spend the money, the ones that are characters. If you need to go around pounding your chest over what a great businessman you are, then you ought to get into to the widget business.

"If you're in sports, it should be about competition and winning. If you're an owner and your only objective is running a good business, really, you should take those principles and be involved in something else. What a league should desire are people who want to compete and win. That's what makes for a great league."

It's also why Colangelo's next conversation with Moreno went like this:

"Remember when we talked a while ago?" Colangelo said.

"Yes," Moreno said.

"I should've sold you the team," Colangelo said.

In the end, baseball did not end the way it should've for Colangelo, the man who shaped Phoenix into a big-league city. But in 2004, it was just a few pages in the darkest chapter of his storybook career.

He sold the Suns. He stepped down from the Diamondbacks. He lost his good friend, Cotton Fitzsimmons, to cancer. He was inducted into the Pro Basketball Hall of Fame. He went on a European vacation, where his wife was mugged and he got into a fight on the streets of Paris.

As Colangelo was exchanging blows with a stranger wearing a motorcycle helmet, two Jewish men in yarmulkes came to help. They were brothers. One was a doctor, one was a lawyer. This is not a joke.

"They got in there and tried to help me," Colangelo said. "The lawyer broke his hand. Thank God it wasn't the doctor."

Now that's a joke.

"I caught some pepper spray in my face, so I was in bad shape. Our plans for the night were over," Colangelo said. "But when we got back to the hotel room, I ordered champagne from room service, I poured my wife a glass and said, 'You know, babe, for two 65-year-olds, we handled ourselves really well.'

"The irony is this: When I got back from Europe, I had a couple of speaking engagements. I related all the incidents, and I said jokingly that what scared me most is that the year wasn't even over yet. And then a few weeks later, there was some additional news."

Doctors discovered Colangelo had prostate cancer. He had successful surgery performed in New York on December 30, in a hospital near Times Square. He spent New Year's Eve recovering in bed.

It was a humbling year that literally knocked Colangelo on his backside. And it was another reason why retirement was out of the question, and why some kind of encore was necessary.

"You could say the call came at the perfect time," Colangelo said.

CHAPTER 4

Roots

• •

Officially, the reformation of American basketball begins here, with a call from NBA headquarters in the spring of 2005. Russ Granik was Stern's deputy commissioner, and wondering if Colangelo would please take over the reigns of Team USA.

The NBA was tired of hearing and reading terrible things about its players, and the 2004 Olympics had left quite a mark. Privately, Stern was seething over Brown's divisive performance in Athens, and how fragile USA Basketball had become.

There was tepid interest among players. The Olympics were now considered a no-win situation, with expectations absurdly high. NBA players didn't easily adapt to the international game, where they employ a strange ball, shorter quarters, and a trapezoidal lane.

It didn't help when Tim Duncan went off during the 2004 Olympics, proclaiming that "FIBA sucks."

Stern desperately needed someone to lead a reclamation project. Someone to cut through the red tape inside USA Basketball, polish up the operation, and most importantly, restore pride in Olympic basketball among the NBA's elite players.

Not many people could pull that off. Even back then, it seemed preordained that a man of Colangelo's stature would be so readily available, physically and emotionally, to accept a heavy, complicated assignment that paid absolutely nothing.

"Russ said the commissioner was very upset," Colangelo said.

Colangelo felt the calling and didn't hesitate, but he made his conditions simple and clear: He needed full autonomy, and he didn't want to be hampered by budget restraints. In return, the NBA would be getting four decades' worth of experience, leadership, fundraising and relationship-building. They would be getting a man who exuded class, a man with an immense international reputation. They would get a leader whose name commanded instant respect in locker rooms across the NBA.

And that means the story of the Olympic team really begins way back here, in a little home in Chicago Heights, made with wood from two railroad box cars.

These days, the house is a historical marker, officially commemorated by the Chicago Heights Historical Association as the boyhood home of Jerry Colangelo. Back in the day, it was just a modest roof over the American dream in the middle of a blue-collar neighborhood.

The house was built by Colangelo's grandparents, immigrants from a mountain village in Italy. It was filled up with extended family trying to lay roots in a new country. Colangelo's room was so small that as he grew to be a star athlete, his feet would extend off his bed and into his younger sister's room.

He lived in a hard-hat community, and learned to improvise. There were times when Colangelo would actually leave the house with a salt shaker in his pocket. When he became hungry, he would pluck a tomato off a neighbor's vine for an impromptu lunch.

He didn't know it at the time, but this upbringing would become part of the inimitable bond Colangelo developed with his players. His boyhood existence resembled the struggles of numerous inner-city players who grew up without fathers, in poverty-stricken areas.

Colangelo knew what it was like under a shaky roof.

"I came from a broken home," he said. "I had a bad relationship with my dad. He had a lot of issues. A lot of things happened in my life with him. Bottom line is, I never played ball with him once, never played catch with him, never shot a basketball with him. So there was nothing."

Then one night, Colangelo came home and found his mother covered with bruises.

He was 17 then, and about to become a man.

"I heard my dad pull up, and then he came stumbling up the stairs," Colangelo said. "And when he hit the top step, I hit him right in the mouth. I warned him to never touch her again. At that moment, he walked out and slept in his car."

Two years later, Colangelo's father ran away from home.

"He took off when I was 19," Colangelo said. "He took off when three guys came looking for him because they were going to kill him. And he was gone."

By then, Colangelo was deeply immersed in athletics. He went to Kansas on a basketball scholarship to play with Wilt Chamberlain. When Chamberlain bolted for the Harlem Globetrotters, Colangelo transferred back home, to the University of Illinois.

Ironically, one of his new teammates at Illinois - Mannie Jackson - would one day own the Globetrotters.

"The thing about Jerry is that he's authentic," Jackson said. "He has a steady hand. He's one of the most generous guys you'll ever meet in your life. He's not a tough guy who will shoot you in the back if you did him wrong.

"But the word I keep coming back to is authenticity. He's always lived what he believes in, and he's been that way since he was 17. Jerry is the same way now as he was when I first met him, back when it was unfashionable to spend time with African-American players.

"A friend and I went through high school and college together, and when we got to that school environment, it was all segregated. We never got socially involved with the other players, and there were very few black kids around. We became very isolated around holiday time. But one time, Jerry came by with a case of beer.

"I had never drank before. We sat there and drank that beer, and talked about philosophy, the future of the world, and what basketball meant to us. Look, I'm worth a lot of money, and I've done a lot of things. But I've never met anyone quite like Jerry Colangelo."

While Colangelo had developed his own sense of values at an early age, he wasn't sure where it was all going after college. And at age 26, he had one of those great moments in life, when a door closes, a window opens and the rest is history.

By now, Colangelo had three children. He had just left his stake in a faltering tuxedo renting/dry cleaning enterprise. His only job was playing semiprofessional basketball at night for $50 a game.

He sat down at the kitchen table. He told his wife, Joan, to go to bed. He began searching through his wallet for business cards, for any job leads he could find. He picked out a card given to him by his father-in-law.

It was a lucky draw.

That card directed Colangelo to Dick Klein, a business owner and Chicago sports fan who wanted nothing more in life than to own his own sports franchise. The two men instantly bonded over basketball, and over time, Colangelo became Klein's point man in the pursuit of an NBA franchise.

Together, they raised $750,000 necessary for entrance into the NBA. But on the day they went to sign papers, the league upped the price another $500,000. Welcome to the big leagues, kid.

"When we got the team, we started thinking about names," Colangelo said. "We were thinking headlines, and how it helps to have a short name. You had the stockyards, where they used to slaughter the bulls. Bulls were vicious animals. Then you think of the town: Bears, Cubs, Sox, Bulls. It fit."

And if you were in downtown Chicago on a certain day in 1966, you would've seen Colangelo at his marketing best, driving up and down Michigan Avenue with a live bull in the back of the flatbed truck.

But it wasn't always paradise. In Year 2, a kid named Walt Frazier was there for the taking in the NBA draft. However, Colangelo knew the fledgling operation didn't have the money to pay a player like Frazier. Remorsefully, he passed him on to the Knicks.

It was exactly the kind of lost opportunity that would rarely happen when Colangelo got his own franchise.

As the NBA expanded, so did Colangelo's marketability. He was recruited to lead a startup franchise in Phoenix. He arrived in the desert with three children, nine suitcases and $300 in his pocket.

"I left O'Hare (airport) and it was 20 below zero," Colangelo said. "I got off the plane, and palm trees were swaying. I inhaled a smell I never experienced before. It was the sweet smell of orange blossoms."

But he was also tough, seasoned and hardened beyond his years. He would serve as general manager, transition into owner, and grow a small-market team out of the desert floor. During Colangelo's time at the wheel, the Suns would compile the fourth-best overall record in NBA history.

He called all the shots. He became the youngest general manager in history. In moments of desperation, he even served as head coach, taking over the position midway through just his second season in Phoenix.

It was a dream scenario for Colangelo. He was only 30, and after replacing Johnny "Red Kerr," he guided the Suns to a 24-20 record over the second half of the season. And then came a surreal road game in Atlanta, where Colangelo left his team in the locker room to watch the preliminary game, just to pass the time.

As he walked by the court, he saw his father's face in the stands. It was a face he hadn't seen in more than a decade.

"I saw him sitting across the way with a woman and a young boy," Colangelo said. "And I turned and went the other way.

"The game is over, and that game clinched a playoff sport for us, so there was some activity on the court. And then an interview. And when I finished all of that, I turned, and there he was, standing on the corner of the floor. He had tears coming down his cheeks."

Colangelo's teams made two great runs at an NBA championship, losing to John Havlicek's Celtics in 1976 and Michael Jordan's Bulls in 1993. Yet it was the structure of the organization that made Colangelo seem special, a culture that made the Suns feel much different than most NBA franchises.

The organization was loaded with ex-players. Loyalty was at a premium. Head coaches were almost always promoted from within the franchise. Colangelo's handshake was an ironclad promise. Everything was done with a first-class kind of feel.

Colangelo was open and accessible. He threw out a welcome mat for the media. His public relations staff became legendary for its accommodating nature. He always returned phone calls. He became rich, but he was never blinded by greed, and never got too full of himself. He still goes back to Chicago Heights just to "put his feet on the ground." He never forgot his roots.

He empowered and listened to his employees. But ultimately, you know who's in charge when he's in the room.

Under Colangelo's watch, the Suns were remarkably consistent, and never short of heartbreak. They lost a coin flip with Milwaukee that cost them the No. 1 pick in the draft. The Bucks took Lew Alcindor. As a consolation prize, the Suns took Neal Walk.

The irony would work on many levels, as Colangelo had also been courted to lead the expansion Bucks before choosing the job in Phoenix. Later, Alcindor would change his name to Kareem Abdul-Jabbar and come west to play for the Lakers, further haunting the Suns.

The 1976 NBA Finals were famously stamped by Garfield Heard's shot heard round the world, and because referee Richie Powers chose not to call an automatic technical foul on the Celtics for signaling for a timeout they didn't possess. The Celtics went on to win Game 6, and the championship. But not without mild protest.

One of John MacLeod's assistant coaches on that team - Al Bianchi - would later purchase his own championship ring and inscribe it, "(Bleep) You, Richie Powers."

Some 11 years later, fans had grown restless, frustrated with the existing ownership group. Colangelo assembled investors, raised $44 million and purchased the Suns from the same men who recruited him to Phoenix: Richard Bloch, Donald Pitt and Donald Diamond.

From 1993-95, Colangelo would get within arm's reach of a championship trophy, only to be disappointed by the focus, commitment and nocturnal antics of Charles Barkley. And while the Lakers segued from Wilt Chamberlain to Abdul-Jabbar to Shaquille O'Neal, Colangelo's teams always seemed to be that one player short, that big center who could make the difference.

During a low ebb for the Suns in the mid-1990s, Colangelo was occasionally criticized for making his son, Bryan, the team's general manager. Bryan was only 34 when he was promoted to team president, and the weight of responsibility wore him down. It got even hotter when a local columnist used words like *silver spoon* and *nepotism* in a piece that ran during the ill-fated Tom Gugliotta/Luc Longley era.

Colangelo tracked down the writer in Australia, and said the distance between them was the only thing saving the writer from Colangelo's fist.

He was kidding. Or so I hoped.

But looking at his life in full, it all made sense. Colangelo loved having his son at his side. He felt guilty about the enormous shadow he cast over Bryan, and once sent him far away to college just so he could become his own man. He loved big gatherings and family functions and the feeling that everyone depended upon him.

It was all because his own dad gave him close to nothing. The man who had no father to speak of became Godfather to everyone under his wing, on his payroll, at his table.

While Colangelo never won a championship with the Suns, Colangelo grew a reputation as a man who rewarded the players, who cared about players. The most famous example is Danny Manning, who turned down a multi-year offer from the Clippers because he wanted to sign with the Suns.

With an overloaded payroll, Colangelo could only offer a one-year deal for $1 million. But he told Manning he was aware of what the player was leaving behind. Those words were heavy with implied promise, and they were as good as gold. They shook hands.

Just 46 games into the following season, Manning blew out his knee during a morning practice. As he lay on the trainer's table, Manning knew he had nothing in writing. He was in a precarious, vulnerable position.

About that time, Colangelo came down from his office, and walked in the trainer's room.

"I remember what you passed up," Colangelo said. "And I never forget."

The next season, Manning had a new $40 million contract.

"To the best of my knowledge, no one else (among owners) started out like I did," Colangelo said. "I ended up promoting, scouting, managing, coaching, owning. It was all done through the system. Usually in ownership, guys make money elsewhere and end up owning a franchise. They didn't do it from within the system. And I always felt I had a little edge over the years because players knew that, too.

"I always had great relationships with the players in the NBA. At times, it was almost embarrassing. During a collective bargaining session, (Knicks center) Patrick Ewing got up and said (to the owners), 'We don't trust any of you. Except for Jerry. We trust him.' That's why my word being my bond along the way has been a great benefit and value to the Phoenix Suns franchise. Because players would do things based just on my word."

There are times when Colangelo pieces together his life, and just shakes his head in amazement. Why did he get such opportunities? How did he become so influential, so well regarded? How did a kid hustling and learning about life on the streets end up eating with presidents and watching gymnasiums and streets become named in his honor?

He calls it God's plan. It keeps him humble. It's the only way it makes sense.

But nothing is perfect. And nearing the end of his career, the Suns have suffered great angst and heartbreak in the pursuit of a championship. There were questionable personnel moves, and the contentious departures of Joe Johnson and Shawn Marion probably wouldn't have happened if Colangelo had been calling the shots.

Then there's the tragic story of his father, who after a lifetime of abandonment, came to Phoenix just in time to say goodbye.

"The sadness is he never got to know my family," Colangelo said. "He missed out on everything. He never got to know my kids until the last five years of his life, when he moved to Arizona and was living in a home. Until he passed. We made peace. But it's sad."

Fortunately, sadness is usually a temporary condition. And now, a basketball championship was within his grasp once again. Colangelo had been waiting 40 years for a team and a moment like this.

CHAPTER 5
Taking Flight
. . . .

Inside the National Italian American Sports Hall of Fame, there is a baseball mitt once worn by Joe DiMaggio. There is a heavyweight belt that belonged to Rocky Marciano. There are headsets worn by Harry Caray.

There is also a telling quote from Mike Eruzione, who scored the game-winning goal against the Russians in 1980, completing the Miracle on Ice:

"Three more inches to the left and I'd be painting bridges."

The museum is located in a small Chicago community dubbed Little Italy, a proud neighborhood known for great restaurants. And if you could've been at the museum on June 25, 2005, you would've seen the history of a sport come to life.

Michael Jordan, Larry Bird and Clyde Drexler showed up.

So did Jerry West, Dean Smith and Lenny Wilkens.

So did John Thompson, Chuck Daly and Scottie Pippen.

Colangelo had invited select players and anyone who had ever coached an Olympic team to be part of the initial brainstorming session. The response was overwhelming, and that night, more than 30 legends arrived in a convoy of limousines. The only Olympic coaches missing were the late Pete Newell, who was having cancer surgery; Larry Brown, who was coaching the Pistons in the NBA Finals; and Bobby Knight, who was away on a fishing trip.

Oscar Robertson and Bill Russell couldn't make it, but pledged their support. Rudy Tomjanovich became ill driving down from Michigan, but sent Colangelo a detailed report.

In his quest to restore the glory, Colangelo found no shortage of friends.

"Look, I was appalled by what I saw in Athens," Colangelo said. "There was such a dislike for Americans, and that really bothered me. But everything we had done was coming right back at us. That had to change. I accepted this job because I cared. I was insulted with the perception of Ugly Americans all over the world. I told everyone that's why I was involved, and how we had a stage to do something very important."

Even without this esteemed company, Colangelo already knew what had to change. There must be one voice leading Team USA, not a bureaucracy that resulted from a series of committee votes. The organization needed to create a national team with a deep well of committed players. USA Basketball had to pick better teams, equipped with more role players. They must somehow practice more often, better, smarter.

Most of all, Colangelo needed to build precious team unity, somehow meshing millionaire athletes over small windows of practice availability during the NBA's off-season. He did the math. He needed a three-year commitment to make that happen.

The number was a big problem. Three years? That's three off-seasons out of a player's career, three summers when a player must forsake rest and risk injury to voluntarily play more high-stress basketball. It came at a time when many of the premier NBA players had bailed on *six-week* commitments to play in Athens.

Three years? That was going to be difficult.

"I appreciate you all being here," Colangelo told the room. "I'd be foolish not to take your input. I want to use you as a sounding board. I want to hear from each of you."

The room full of giants did more than give Colangelo knowledge. They gave him leverage. In the end, they would endorse his plan, help form his plan. That would be a powerful recruiting tool, if needed, when assembling his team.

After Colangelo spoke, former players and coaches shared their Olympic experiences, good and bad. Then Colangelo solicited advice on potential coaches, and those in attendance voiced their opinions candidly.

They compiled a list featuring all the prominent names: Duke coach Mike Krzyzewski, Lousville coach Rick Pitino, Spurs coach Gregg Popovich, Knicks coach Mike D'Antoni, Portland coach Nate McMillan, Syracuse coach Jim Boeheim, etc.

Everyone in the room was given a vote. Krzyzewski and Popovich finished in a dead heat. The coach with the third-most votes was a write-in candidate, the retired Pat Riley.

This was a dilemma. Popovich had earned the chance. He had served USA Basketball from 2002-04, working under Larry Brown and George Karl. He brought a handful of championship rings to the table, and a whole lot more.

The Spurs obviously excelled at scouting international players. Popovich graduated from the Air Force Academy, and worked overseas as an intelligence officer. He understood the essence of patriotism. He knew enough about the global dynamics of basketball to take the word "World" off the Spurs' championship banners.

As a coach, Popovich is open-minded yet very much in control. He strikes a great balance between toughness and humor. He knows how to motivate and prod his players without getting personal. During the 2003 Tournament of the Americas, he bragged so much about Argentina's team that his own players began to seethe. And when the two teams met in the title game, the Americans were out for blood. They beat the Argentinians, 106-73.

While Popovich has become an icon in San Antonio, he is also a master at striking down individual egos. He likes it very much when players *get over themselves*. He specializes in fostering real team chemistry.

"He has a policy that if he ever runs into a player in a restaurant, he automatically picks up the tab," said Steve Kerr, former member of the Spurs. "So one night, Danny Ferry and I decide to go out to eat in Seattle. We ask the concierge for recommendations, and he tells us to go to this seafood restaurant. He tells us it's the same one our coach is going to later that night."

Kerr and Ferry looked at each other, smelling the fish and an opportunity.

"We said, 'Perfect. This will be a free meal,' " Kerr said. "So we get there an hour before he did. We had a good meal. We go up and wait by the front of the restaurant, where there's a giant revolving door.

"Pop walks in with his staff at 8:15. His reservation was for 8:00. As soon as he comes out of the revolving door, I walk by and hand him the check. Danny says to him, 'It's about time you got here. You're 15 minutes late. We have a movie to catch.' And just like that, we were in the revolving door going the other way. Pop loved that one."

Colangelo knew all about Popovich, who had grown into one of the NBA's true impact coaches. Pop's Spurs had been beating Colangelo's Suns for years. But he also felt a magnetic presence and freshness about Krzyzewski, who had played for Bobby Knight at West Point and turned Duke basketball into an NCAA power. Krzyzewski came with more polish, more passion, and a more collegial feel. His communication skills were outstanding. His coaching was already structured around 40-minute games, the same length as Olympic basketball.

There were other elements to consider. Without Popovich, Colangelo had virtually no chance to recruit Spurs star Tim Duncan, who had lashed out at Olympic basketball during the 2004 fiasco. On the other hand, Lakers star Kobe Bryant had long fantasized about playing for Krzyzewski, and there would be great synergy between coach and star player.

In the end, it was Colangelo's call, just like the Diamondbacks over the Scorpions.

Like Colangelo, Krzyzewski also came from Chicago. The two men came from the same world. They spoke the same language. They felt comfortable with each other. And during this meeting of legends in their hometown, Krzyzewski received an unlikely endorsement.

"If there's one college coach who can get the job done, it's Mike Krzyzewski," said former North Carolina coach Dean Smith.

The room went silent. Tobacco Road must've buckled. A Tar Heel was endorsing a Blue Devil. The irony of the moment was lost on no one. It was the final piece of affirmation Colangelo needed.

"It was an amazing thing to hear," Colangelo said.

Before making his decision official, Colangelo would have a phone conversation with Popovich about the job. He immediately sensed that Popovich seemed tired of the process, embittered by what went down in Athens. He didn't feel the same energy that he felt from Krzyzewski.

Deep down, Colangelo knew whom he wanted as a partner, even if it would cause some friction with Popovich down the line.

"He felt I misrepresented a phone conversation when I spoke with him," Colangelo said. "I just sensed that he was not as enthusiastic about the job unless we went and changed a lot of things. I just didn't feel any energy or desire coming from him. Even though I've said many positive things about Pop, he didn't feel I read him the right way.

"All I can say is this: I was hiring my partner for the next three years, and Coach K was ready to jump through the phone. I had a clear choice in my mind."

Before the limousines disbanded into the night, there was one final matter of business. They went over every position on the court, from shooting guard to defensive stopper. They laughed at how the United States had to adapt to foreign rules in a game Americans once invented. That didn't seem fair.

Then they started naming names.

They put 50 players on the board. Colangelo made it clear that he didn't want an all-star team, a rotisserie team or a team that looked good on paper. He wanted role players, chemistry, character and heart. He wanted grit and he wanted gold. He wanted the future to look like the past.

He wanted passion by the bucketful, and across the room, one of the legends began to stir.

CHAPTER 6
Mr. Clutch

· ·

The NBA logo is the silhouette of an old-time player. His hair is cropped short, well above the ears. He's earthbound, dribbling the ball with his left hand, and not appearing to move very fast. His right arm is cocked at the elbow, as if to shield an invisible defender.

Sometimes Jerry West puts on a pair of NBA socks, sees that logo and smiles at the caricature of himself.

It's like looking in the mirror and seeing another generation.

"The commissioner doesn't want to say that's me, but all indications are that it's me," said West. "They probably don't want to pay me a royalty. But if that is me, then I'm very proud of it. It's almost like I'm wearing my own apparel."

West doesn't like talking about the logo. He's aware that some people think it's out of touch, that it doesn't represent today's NBA. He knows that some members of the media have lobbied for change, wanting to replace West's dribble drive with the silhouette of a leaping Michael Jordan.

"If the league would be served by a better logo, so be it," West said.

Not a chance.

While extremely private and almost reclusive, West will always be one of basketball's great ambassadors. His humility is legendary, and his honesty and toughness aren't far behind. He was an All-Star in each of his 14 seasons. He broke his nose nine times. No one ever heard him complain.

He was the rural boy from West Virginia who made it all the way to Hollywood. His jump shot was poetry and art. His touch in the clutch was legendary.

"At the end of games, he was like Kobe Bryant," said former Pistons center Bob Lanier. "Or I should say, Kobe is now like Jerry West."

West was also a perfectionist, tormented by failure. He won only one championship as a member of the Lakers, and the 13 years that passed without a trophy have "left a lot of scars." He never took credit for victories and never posed after making big shots, not even after the miraculous buzzer-beater from beyond halfcourt that forced overtime in Game 3 of the 1970 NBA Finals.

Watch the video. West acts like he *should've* made that shot.

He would be as out of place in the 21st century NBA as the short shorts he's wearing in the logo.

"I'm a very solitary person," West said. "I don't do very many things to draw attention to myself."

But this night in Chicago was different. The Olympics still set his heart aglow. Back when he played, the jersey was an honor and a privilege. West was only 13 when he lost his brother in the Korean War, and so the flag meant something special. The idea of playing for his country was intensely personal.

"You have to look at what has happened to America," West said. "The sense of nationalism isn't as great as it used to be. I think when you lose that, when it's not that important to play for your country, then something is seriously wrong. I had a brother who gave his life for this country."

At the time, West was also part of the best Olympic team ever assembled. The 1960 squad of college and amateur players was so perfectly balanced that five of them averaged double-figure scoring. Ten of them went on to play in the NBA, most notably West, Oscar Robertson and Jerry Lucas. They were coached by Pete Newell. They were so good that

John Havlicek could only make the team as an alternate. Their average margin of victory was more than 42 points per game.

The 1960 Olympics also carried great historical significance. They were staged in Rome, inside a Cold War, with heightened tensions between the United States and the Soviet Union. They represented the rise of great female athletes, particularly Wilma Rudolph. They served up the debut of a kid named Cassius Clay, and the world would never be the same.

Along the way, the basketball team simply pounded the competition, setting up a semifinal match with the Russians, which featured a 7-foot-3, 320-pound woodcutter named Jan Kruminsh. The arena was overflowing with fans. In a pre-game speech, the American players were told that a victory over the Russians would be a victory over communism, and that a loss would be devastating, just like that American spy plane that had been shot down over Russia.

The game was stuffed with propaganda and national pride. The Russians kept it close, trailing only 35-28 at halftime. And then West took over. Team USA scored 20 points in the first five minutes of the second half, blowing open a close game.

The Americans followed with a gold-medal victory over Brazil, extending America's Olympic winning streak to 36 games. It remains one of the proudest moments in West's life.

"Walk into my house in California, and you'll find a couple paintings of me," West said. "And in this room, there's my Olympic gold medal, my uniform and a picture of that team proudly displayed. Those are my only real significant pieces of memorabilia."

West isn't joking. It was once reported that the game ball from his 25,000[th] point in the NBA ended up as a pickup ball used in the family driveway.

It is also why he was hurt more than most by what had happened to Team USA, and why he was one of the night's most passionate contributors.

"It's as if we were lost in the forest," West said. "There were plenty of trees, with the trees being the players, but we didn't know where to go. I was embarrassed. I mean, really embarrassed, OK? It was like a cancer had crept in the process.

"There are a few things that have stunted the growth of the league and our basketball players, and some of it is a lack of appreciation. A lot of the young kids coming into the NBA don't have the experience or the knowledge of how different the game once was. It certainly isn't a lack of athletic ability.

"A lot of these kids who are drafted early, some are the most incredible athletes you'll ever see. But they don't understand the essence of the team game. They have been sponsored by shoe companies that market the flamboyant parts of the game, the dunks and the highlight reel stuff. It's pretty to watch and all. But it's not the essence of the game. It's not the nuts and bolts of basketball.

"Problem is, there are a lot of distractions these days, things that promote something other than good teamwork. Today, you get agents asking NBA general managers when their guy is going to get a chance to play. The answer is, when they deserve to."

Before West became an NBA icon, he was a hard-nosed kid, the son of a coal mine electrician. He fell in love with basketball out in the country, alone but not lonely, content to spend hours in a dirt driveway, shooting at a rim affixed to a storage shed.

West practiced in the rain until his shoes were covered with mud. He practiced in the winter with gloves on both hands. That ball was literally his best friend, no matter what pain it caused.

"I can remember my hands bleeding because the skin would be so cracked," West said.

West built his stamina by running into the nearest town of Cabin Creek, just to pick up the family mail. He had a vivid imagination. And out in that driveway by himself, he did what every basketball player has ever done.

"I would become the coach, the referee, the general manager and the player," West said. "I'd play mind games. I'd create situations and take the last-second shot. And you never let yourself miss that shot, even if you have to figure out a way to put another second back on the clock."

After he retired, West became a celebrated talent evaluator and team builder. He boldly selected Vlade Divac with the 26th pick in the first round of the 1989 NBA Draft, and was richly rewarded. He identified and traded for a kid named Kobe Bryant. The dynasty he never knew as a player occurred under his watch as a general manager.

He is possibly the best combination of player and executive in the history of the game, and inside the meeting room in Chicago, his words rang heavy and true.

"To me, character counts," West said. "I really didn't want players that were troubled or needed extra special attention. If you have that player on your team who is only creating conversation and controversy, I never found that palatable.

"I know what makes teams win, OK? There's an order to it. You need stars to carry you and win the big games. You need players who fill distinct roles. Most of the individual things you see in the NBA today, they're not the nuts and bolts of what basketball is all about. But every year, the champion is composed of tough, hard-minded kids who play the game the right way, defend, pass the ball and remain unselfish."

West said his peace, and would exit the game two years later. While he led the Grizzlies to three consecutive playoff appearances, he couldn't work the same magic in Memphis as he did in Los Angeles.

After West retired, the Grizzlies shipped Pau Gasol to the Lakers in a controversial, cost-cutting trade. The deal instantly transformed Los Angeles into a championship contender, and attracted much criticism.

Popovich said it was "beyond comprehension," adding that the NBA should have a committee in place to veto imbalanced trades. The deal was so lopsided that some believed West had to be involved, steering Gasol to the franchise he once served and loved.

It wasn't true. And it shrouded the bigger message involved:

A diverse, intelligent big man from Spain had tipped the balance of power in the NBA.

"You hear it all the time. Basketball is America's game. No, it's not," West said. "It's not America's game anymore. It's a worldwide game. And somewhere in China or some other little place on the map, there's a young Jerry West out there, shooting until his hands bleed, doing the same things."

CHAPTER 7
Playing for Mo
....

The hotel room in Santo Domingo was nothing special. It was a two-star accommodation with two beds, and far too little space for the 20 people jammed inside.

Jerry Colangelo, new leader of Team USA, had summoned everyone for an impromptu meeting. He ditched the victory speech. He dug deep into his pockets.

"Look, I'm going to give you 10 grand," Colangelo said. "This is an incentive."

He threw the money on the bed. Silence filled the room.

"Split it up. It's yours," Colangelo said. "But we've got to qualify."

Heard of the Dream Team? This was the Transition Team, a rag-tag group of basketball players thrown together in the wake of the Athens debacle, a team promptly dispatched to the 2005 FIBA Americas Championship in the Dominican Republic.

While Colangelo tried to put USA Basketball back on the rails for the long term, the immediate mission was to qualify for the 2006 World Championships in Japan. It wasn't going to be easy. It wasn't going to be pretty.

In the grand sweep of history, this was rock bottom.

"USA Basketball didn't have any money, and I knew I had to do something," Colangelo said. "Can you imagine the USA not in the World Championships after what happened in Athens?"

There were some familiar names who jumped at a chance to play for their country, like Charlie Bell, a member of the "Flint-stones" trio that won an NCAA championship at Michigan State; Lynn Greer, a gifted scorer who played for John Chaney at Temple; and Tyus Edney, the diminutive guard from UCLA who once raced 94 feet with the ball, scoring at the buzzer and eliminating Missouri in the NCAA Tournament.

The rest were a compilation of CBA players, development league players and players currently working in Europe. They were Kris Lang, Aaron McGhee, Alex Scales, Jerome Beasley, Ron Slay, Tang Hamilton, Marque Perry, Noel Felix and Adam Chubb.

They were a long way from home. And from a quality standpoint, they were light years away from the Dream Team that sparked a global revolution.

Nonetheless, they needed to spare America any further embarrassment. They needed to play hard, keep their mouths shut and deal with the toxic climate.

The top four finishers in the 10-nation event automatically qualified for the World Championship in Japan. An at-large bid would also be awarded down the line, and would probably go to the Americans, if absolutely necessary. But given the anti-American sentiment in 2005, no one wanted to take that chance. And, certainly, no one wanted to endure the ridicule that would come with such an act of charity.

That 10 grand on the bed was a sign of desperation. It was also an investment that could save USA Basketball a mountain of bad publicity.

"Mr. Colangelo came in and said, 'You guys are sacrificing a lot. I'm going to sacrifice something, too,' " Bell said. "He was telling us that if we go out and get the job done, we won't be forgotten. What we were doing was greatly appreciated."

Not many people knew about this team. Not many wanted to know about this team. Playing for Team USA had become a high-risk, low-reward endeavor. It came with zero pay, and if things didn't go well, it guaranteed a mob of angry fans.

It wasn't very appealing to coaches either, and USA Basketball trudged back to the doorstep of Morris "Mo" McHone, a veteran coach who specialized in organized chaos, in shaping mercenary teams on the fly.

"One of the things I've always known is that when USA Basketball calls me, they're having a hard time putting together an NBA team," McHone said. "I'm the kind of guy ... I don't get to coach those really good teams."

McHone talks with a Southern twang, and his resume• is long. He graduated from Florida State in 1965. He became a college assistant, a trusted wing man for the legendary Hugh Durham. He worked in Korea. He worked in the National Basketball Development League. He became a sizzling hot CBA commodity for a short time, reaching the finals with four different teams in a five-year span. He once stepped in for Stan Albeck, and went 11-21 as head coach of the Spurs.

Then he stepped down, where he's a lot more comfortable. But he's always answered the bell for USA Basketball.

"I've done it three times for my country," McHone said. "And this last time was definitely the hardest. We had 18 commitments from guys who said they would play. Out of those 18 originally invited, only three showed up."

McHone was assisted by former Celtics great Dennis Johnson and former DePaul coach Joey Meyer. They set up training camp at the Heat's facility in Miami, and stayed at the Marriott Residence Inn. Their roster didn't include many big players, and offered little interior presence. But no one dared complain. No one said a word.

They were just thankful they had enough players to field a team.

"We were scrambling for players until the end," McHone said. "It was totally unfair to the players we were calling, but they were so happy to have an opportunity. They were the kind of guys, you call them one day and they're on the plane the next day to Miami. NBA guys can't fit this into their schedules. These guys didn't have schedules."

After a week of preparation, they left for a series of exhibition games in Brazil. Team USA lost four of five games, including all three games against Brazil. Once, they played in a sweltering gym located inside a health club. Another time, they played at an arena so new that the cement was still curing outside.

This Team USA was not like a traveling rock band. To outsiders, the only real celebrity in the bunch was Dennis Johnson. He was DJ from the Celtics dynasty, once called the greatest teammate ever by the great Larry Bird. Things were so bad that an assistant coach was the star of the group, and the locals had Johnson leave hand prints in the wet cement outside the main entrance.

When Johnson died two years later, suffering a heart attack while playing pickup basketball at the age of 52, that impromptu monument became something special.

"It was tough because everyone was looking at us like we were the Dream Team," Bell said. "Anytime you've got that USA on your chest, people are shooting for you. We were a team of guys who played in Europe, but they acted like they were playing against Jordan, Pippen and Kobe, and they were celebrating when they beat us."

The thrill of throttling the once-powerful Americans had not grown old. Yet while they lacked height and transcendent talent, this Team USA had some fight. They showed up in the Dominican Republic for the start of the real tournament, and promptly spanked Panama, 94-72.

Then they played Brazil again, for keeps. Leandro Barbosa, then a quality role player for the Suns, couldn't be stopped. He scored 37 points, but the Americans wouldn't budge. The teams exchanged leads three times in the final minute. And after Barbosa converted a layup and free throw, the Brazilians led 94-93 with 6.4 seconds left.

McHone called timeout. He wanted the ball in Greer's hands, and he wanted penetration. But Greer took the first open window. He pulled up from beyond the three-point arc, drawing a controversial foul. Greer was awarded three free throws. The crowd was stunned. The Americans had a chance to steal the game.

The crowd began jeering. Brazil's bench was going crazy on the referees. McHone couldn't believe his eyes, or his ears.

"In the NBA, we would've lost that game because they would have not called that foul," McHone said. "Here, he goes up to shoot, the guy hits his hand, and it's a foul. I was shocked they made that call."

With all that chaos swirling in the air, Greer looked over at McHone.

"Coach, I got it," he said.

Greer was a Philadelphia high school legend, finishing two slots behind Wilt Chamberlain on the city's list of all-time prep scoring leaders. He endured John Chaney's infamous 5:30 a.m. practices, and averaged 23.2 points per game as a senior.

He once laid 47 points on Wisconsin in Madison. During the semifinals of the A-10 Tournament, he once stepped to the line and sank three consecutive free throws with three seconds left, eliminating George Washington, 76-74. He had some nerve, this kid.

Now, he stepped up, and did the very same thing.

Swish. Swish. Swish.

"He came through (John) Chaney, so you know the kid was tough," McHone said. "But I'm telling you, there was stuff going all around, people walking everywhere, and the net didn't move on any of them. From there on out, I had a tremendous respect for Lynn Greer."

Alas, Team USA was soon exposed. They lost to Canada. They were unable to get a shot off on the final possession in a one-point loss to Venezuela. They were smoked by Argentina. They caught a big break in the standings when Panama - coached by former Arkansas boss Nolan Richardson - upset Puerto Rico. And after all the drama and cash incentives, it came down to a must-win game against winless Uruguay to secure a top four finish.

It should've been easy. It wasn't. Team USA should not struggle with Uruguay, ever. But they did. They were losing 63-52 in the final moments of the third quarter. With the ball and 14 seconds remaining, Uruguay had all the momentum, and was milking the clock for a final shot.

It all changed in a matter of seconds. Uruguay was called for an offensive foul. Bell buried a long three-point shot just before the buzzer. In between quarters, Uruguay's bench was called for a technical foul. Bell made a free throw, and then drained another three-point shot on the ensuing possession.

Small moments lead to big victories, and with that spark, Team USA pulled away in the fourth quarter. Bell and Greer did most of the damage, but the team defense was spectacular, forcing desperation shots and consecutive shot clock violations from Uruguay.

After Team USA's 91-77 victory, the Uruguay head coach blamed the loss on "scandalous" officials. It was further proof of how far the Americans had to go to restore their prominence and image, on court and off. But in the other locker room, McHone exhaled deeply.

The Americans would not medal. They would lose their final three games of the tournament. They would get slapped silly in their last game against Brazil. But they had qualified for the World Championship in Japan. They avoided another public relations disaster.

It was the first step on the long road back.

"I was so relieved when we qualified," McHone said. "It's not like my name is a household name. Nobody knows who I am. But nobody feels more connected to Team USA than me.

"All that time in the Dominican Republic, people kept asking me why we weren't bringing our best players. I told them, 'You don't want me to have all my good players. If I did, it wouldn't be much of a tournament. You want to talk about Shaq and Kobe. But you really don't want them to come. Trust me on that.' "

The Transition Team didn't come home to a parade. But to a man, they were all proud of what they had accomplished. Bell even put his jersey in a glass frame, hanging it up in his basement. And ironically, he and Greer would be great teammates once again.

In September 2007, Bell leveraged a two-year, $7 million offer to play for Olympiakos in Greece into a five-year, $18 million deal with the Milwaukee Bucks. That meant Olympiakos still needed a guard, and after successfully requesting his release from the Bucks, Greer accepted the same offer that Bell turned down.

Both players had struck it rich. They had come a long way from staking a share in that 10 grand on the bed.

"Even though we didn't win all our games, we went out there, we played hard, we wanted to be there, and people took notice of that," Bell said. "We took pride in playing for our country. I'd like to think we got the ball rolling again.

"And tell Mr. Colangelo that if he needs a zone buster for the next Dream Team, he should give me a call. I'll even pay for my own plane ticket."

CHAPTER 8
On the Trail

J erry Colangelo rarely dresses casual. He almost always wears a jacket. He has a great sense of style. He returns every phone call. He handles his business in a certain way.

His image is both power, and powerful. And on a superficial level, there's another reason for his unquestioned reputation among the majority of NBA players:

Two of the most beloved films in the hip-hop culture are "Scarface" and "The Godfather." Remove the criminal and gangster elements, take the anti- from the hero, and Colangelo fits the lead archetype perfectly.

He is a self-made man, all the way from rags to riches. He is strong, stoic, and in charge. He cuts a large swath. He can be sentimental, he can lose his temper, but he never loses control. He once ate dinner with President George W. Bush at a Mexican restaurant in Phoenix, and without question, Colangelo looked like the most important man at the table.

He looked like the big boss should, and near the end of the 2008 Olympics, members of the Team USA family would lovingly whisper the same words anytime Colangelo entered the room:

"The Godfather's here."

He was exactly the kind of boss a new generation of players could easily respect, the kind who makes offers you can't refuse. And the first stop was Washington, D.C.

"The first guy I met with was Carmelo Anthony," Colangelo said. "He was nervous. But he ate well. We had a big-time breakfast."

Colangelo's recruiting trail began with a pop, not a bang. His first two candidates were the enigmatic Anthony and the mercurial Gilbert Arenas. He didn't mince words.

Anthony was a special case. He could bust zones with his jump shot. His explosive bursts of offense could change the momentum of games. Plus, he was really good friends with LeBron James, whom Colangelo most certainly needed.

"I told him, 'A lot of people think I'm wasting my time even considering you,' Colangelo said. "'And quite honestly, your performance at the last Olympics was abominable, and it showed to me that you were very immature. But I'll tell you what. You've got the talent and I like your toughness. If you want to be considered, I'll wipe the slate clean. And I'll be watching you all year. And we'll see.'"

From that point on, Anthony shined. Twice during the season, he called Colangelo, just to check in, just to remain in good graces.

"He was too young to be in Athens," Colangelo said.

In Chicago, Colangelo set up a 9 a.m. meeting with James at the Ritz Carlton Hotel. He arrived a few minutes early, taking a seat on a lobby couch. This was going to be interesting.

Colangelo knew that the third-place finish in Athens grated on James, and that the failure would always be on his resumé. Upon returning home, the nickname "LeBronze" soon began to surface. None of it was his fault.

While James received very little playing time in Athens, he always seemed to make an impact. He took over games. He was the best player on the court. And then he was back on the end of the bench.

The sour legacy of that team affected James more than most other young Olympians. In basketball context, James may eventually surpass

Michael Jordan as the best basketball player in history. But he'll never be unbeaten in Olympic play. That's a shame.

At 9 a.m. sharp, the elevator doors opened. It was James and his agent. Colangelo began talking.

James stopped him halfway through

"I'm in," James said. "I'm in. I'm in. I'm in."

Colangelo began to swell with pride. His plan was working.

Later that day, Colangelo had a meeting with Michael Redd. The Bucks' star offered to drive down from Milwaukee, about 100 miles away, after finishing practice.

Colangelo heard a knock on the door of his hotel suite. Redd was wearing a sweat suit and carrying a garment bag. He had one request before the interview began.

"Can I used the bathroom?" Redd asked.

He came out a few minutes later dressed in a suit and tie.

"That was impressive," Colangelo said.

Redd had a small problem with the three-year commitment. He was scheduled to marry his high school sweetheart the following summer, and would miss most of the initial camp. If he made the cut, they would have to find another zone buster for the 2006 World Championship in Japan.

"That's the good thing about being in charge," Colangelo said. "You can use your discretion."

Back in Phoenix, Colangelo met with Heat stars Dwyane Wade and Shaquille O'Neal.

Wade came from the South Side of Chicago, just like Colangelo. It was not a hard sell.

"Mr. Colangelo told me I'd be one of the key parts going forward, and I was excited that he came to me and expressed that face to face," Wade said. "The only thing I needed to hear was that it would be different than 2004. Once I heard that, I was in."

O'Neal was another matter.

In 2001, Colangelo had chaired a rules committee that examined declining television ratings and a dip in league attendance. There was strong evidence that the game had lost its fluidity, and to some extent, its allure.

Colangelo and many others in the NBA wanted more offense and less standing around. The changes were pushed through shockingly fast, and suddenly, teams could play zone defense; they had only eight seconds to get the ball across half court; and three-second violations could be called on defensive players camping in the lane.

Naturally, O'Neal thought the rule was passed just to contain him. He even threatened to retire.

"The head of the committee must be a guy who doesn't have good big-men recruiting skills," O'Neal said. "Bet you if I was on his team, he wouldn't be trying to enforce the rules."

Ah, but O'Neal was wrong on that one. Those subtle changes reversed six years of a downward trend in team scoring. The excruciating isolation game that permeated the NBA - where the three other offensive players did their best to hide on any given play - had all but disappeared.

"Shaq came in thinking he was 100 percent against playing," Colangelo said. "When he left, he was 50-50."

That was just fine, as the meeting with O'Neal was mostly out of professional courtesy. Colangelo's key player was Bryant, who had been feuding with O'Neal for a number of years. The last thing Colangelo wanted was needless, unproductive drama in the locker room. He wanted total focus, not the zoo that would come with a Shaq-Kobe reunion.

By happenstance, Colangelo's meeting with Bryant came right after the Lakers' star dropped 81 points on the Nuggets in January 2006, notching the second highest individual output in NBA history. It was a performance that had the nation buzzing.

"I decided to mess with him just a little bit," Colangelo said. "I looked him in the eye and said, 'What if I said to you that we just want you to pass the ball?' "

Bryant didn't blink.

"I'll do whatever you want," he said.

After that, it was easy. Colangelo had received three-year commitments from the game's best young players - Bryant, James and Wade - and almost everyone wanted on board now. Team USA was quickly stocking the shelves of its first national team, blending older guys for experience and younger guys for the future.

Which is why Colangelo reached out to a 19-year-old phenomenon named Dwight Howard, just an immature rookie in 2004-05.

"I put in a call, but the day went by, and I never got a call back," Colangelo said.

That night, Colangelo's phone rang. It was Dwight Howard's father.

"Mr. Colangelo, this is Dwight Howard Sr.," the voice said. "Did junior call you today?"

"Not yet," Colangelo said.

"He'll call you tomorrow morning," Howard Sr. said. "Is that OK?"

"That's fine," Colangelo said. "And while I have you on the line, I must compliment you and your wife for doing such a wonderful job. Your son is classy young man."

"We're not done yet," came the response.

With all the interest among the NBA's elite, it was clear that a few really good players weren't going to make the cut. Some helped the process along.

Down the road, Shawn Marion simply ejected himself from the conversation. At the time, he was disgruntled with the Suns organization for dangling his name in the trade market and for other instances of perceived mistreatment. He stopped showing up, and was bounced from the squad in the summer of 2007.

Entering the summer of 2008, Stoudemire couldn't bring himself to commit. He said he wanted to rest his troubled knees, and make sure he was healthy for the upcoming 2008-09 season. It was a disappointing outcome for Colangelo, who could never get a straight answer from a player he had drafted out of high school in 2002.

Stoudemire once represented the cunning of Colangelo at its best. When the Suns worked out Stoudemire before the 2002 Draft, Colangelo sat in the stands, spellbound. Stoudemire was raw, unpolished and he couldn't shoot a lick. But he had the ferocity and the naked ambition. Colangelo saw a young Connie Hawkins, and he could relate to a hard-nosed kid who lost his father at age 12, a kid who had to find his own way in the world.

Colangelo told Stoudemire's agent that the Suns planned on selecting the prep star with the No. 9 pick, if he was still available. And he would really appreciate if Stoudemire went into hiding, canceling the rest of his workouts.

He assumed Stoudemire wanted to be part of global history, part of Colangelo's history.

When he declined, Colangelo bit his tongue.

Then there was the outburst from Arenas, who didn't make the team that would compete at the World Championship in Japan, and reacted very badly.

"I just hope people start looking at my basketball talent and stop prejudging me," Arenas told reporters. "Whether it was barely getting a scholarship out of high school or going in the second round of the draft or almost not making the All-Star Game last year, it just always seems like people don't want to give me what I've earned. It's frustrating. I guess I just have to keep working on my game so people have no choice but to recognize me."

Arenas then vowed to extract revenge on Mike D'Antoni and Nate McMillan, two Team USA assistants who also led NBA teams.

"I'm going to be the silent assassin this year," Arenas continued. "I can't wait to play the Suns and Portland. Against Portland, Nate McMillan, I'm going to try to score 100 points in two games. And against D'Antoni, I'm going to try to score 100 in two games. I'm going to try."

A couple months later, Arenas apologized for the reckless comments. And for the record, Arenas scored 54 and 31 points in two games against D'Antoni's Suns the following season. He scored 19 and 9 in two losses against McMillan's Trail Blazers.

Along the road to Beijing, there was one pleasant surprise. Jason Kidd, the veteran point guard, was not in play at the start of the recruiting process. He was going through a nasty divorce. His situation at home wasn't exactly ideal.

But in 2007, Kidd got the itch. His agent called Colangelo, asking what his client's chances were of making the team.

"I told him, 'We'll see,' " Colangelo said.

Very few players ever left the Suns organization harboring ill will for Colangelo and his family. Kidd was the exception. He was traded after the 2000-01 season, after a highly publicized domestic abuse incident with his wife, Joumana.

Joumana had called 911. She complained to the operator that her husband had struck her in the face. Kidd was arrested, and soon he apologized to everyone. He seemed contrite. He underwent counseling. He thought he had made good. But Colangelo never forgot the sight of his own battered mother, and had zero tolerance for this kind of stuff.

Kidd was traded for Stephon Marbury. Kidd claimed he heard about the move while listening to the radio, in a drive-thru line waiting for fast food. For the longest time, he carried a lot of bitterness.

"Before we played Phoenix, I was driving down Route 17 to the Meadowlands, thinking that a lot of players get back at their old teams by scoring a lot of points," Kidd told *New York Magazine*. "I dreamed of beating Phoenix and getting *no* points."

Yet Colangelo is not a man who holds grudges. Down the road, he would see a distinct need for an experienced point guard and some serious veteran leadership. Kidd would become a vital member of Team USA, and he and Colangelo would grow close once again.

"Jason had become the grisly veteran," Colangelo said. "He conducted himself extremely well. He's grown up as a man, and I'm happy to see growth in someone's life.

"The reality is, when these players come into the league, they're young. You can't ever forget that. They're prone to making mistakes, on the court and in life. Some do, and some don't. But you have to ride through those peaks and valleys. You have to forgive and forget. Life's too short."

In the end, Tim Duncan and Kevin Garnett did not want to play. They had already served their country. But there was no shortage of talent in the room, and here's the official list of players who gave something to the cause from 2006-2008:

Bryant; James; Wade; Anthony; Bosh; Howard; Redd; Williams; Stoudemire; Kidd; Arenas; Marion; Tayshaun Prince; Chris Paul; Carlos Boozer; Joe Johnson; Kirk Hinrich; Shane Battier; Chauncey Billups; Bruce Bowen; Elton Brand; Tyson Chandler; Nick Collison; Kevin Durant; Antawn Jamison; Brad Miller; Mike Miller; Adam Morrison; Greg Oden; Lamar Odom; Paul Pierce; J.J. Redick; and Luke Ridnour..

The head coach was going to be one lucky guy.

CHAPTER 9

Special K

· ·

When he was a boy, they called him Mickey. Mike Krzyzewski was the son of Polish immigrants, and the leader of his own street gang. His peers had funny nicknames like Moe, Twams, Porky, Sels, and Trav. They traveled as a pack, and played basketball all over Chicago's northwest side. The guys always followed Mickey's lead, and Mickey always seemed to be going somewhere.

After all these years, nothing has changed.

In high school, Krzyzewski listened to his parents chide him for a week after he turned down an offer to West Point, and then he changed his mind. He played for and learned from Bob Knight. He took over Duke basketball in 1980, and within 12 years, his program was the best in North Carolina.

Tobacco Road would never be the same.

"When I was being recruited, I was a big North Carolina fan," said Grant Hill. "I did not want to go to Duke. But I made a visit. I spent 48 hours on campus, and a lot of it with him. He sold me. And that's his genius.

"What makes him so special, so unique, and a Hall of Fame coach is his ability to get people to buy in, to get people to believe. I don't know if it was his experience at West Point, where those principles about being in a foxhole come to life. But some people can't coach talent. He's great with talent. He's great at getting everyone to sacrifice for that one common goal, which is a lot easier said than done."

During Hill's era, Duke basketball was the underdog, the boys in white hats. In 1991, the Blue Devils avenged a 30-point loss in the previous NCAA title game by stunning unbeaten UNLV in the semifinals. That victory snapped UNLV's 45-game winning streak, and Krzyzewski's team would go on to win its first title.

But it was Duke's poise in its second encounter with the bully that transcended the sport, and made America cheer.

The following season, Duke repeated as NCAA champions, again offering the perfect Kodak moment. This one came on the final play of overtime in the regional final against Kentucky, a play that seemed to symbolize everything about Duke basketball.

The Blue Devils trailed by one point, and with just under three seconds left, they had time for a desperation shot. But they had to travel the length of the floor. The distance made it nearly impossible. Yet in the huddle, Krzyzewski acted as if his victory was a certainty, as if he were diagraming a layup drill.

He said he needed someone to make a pass. He looked at Hill, whose father, Calvin, was once an NFL star.

"I had the football genes," Hill said.

Kentucky coach Rick Pitino left Hill unguarded under the Duke basket. Hill threw an 80-foot pass that was snagged out of the air by Christian Laettner just beyond the free-throw line. Laettner's turnaround shot went in as time expired, and bedlam ensued. It capped a perfect day for the Duke center, who was 10-for-10 from the field and 10-for-10 from the free-throw line.

The play symbolized Duke's pedigree, grit and impenetrable self-belief. It illustrated the Blue Devils' uncanny ability under chaos. It made Krzyzewski's team seem unworldly, unbeatable. It made the program seem too good.

When Duke won a third title in 2001, Krzyzewski fatigue was definitely setting in. Coaches complained that Duke received preferential treatment from the referees. The perception was that Duke had smarter players, and thereby received the benefit of the doubt.

Other coaches complained about media favoritism shown to Krzyzewski's team, and Arizona coach Lute Olson once blistered ESPN announcer Dick Vitale during a press conference, calling him, "Dukie Vitale."

Others claimed that Krzyzewski's polished image was a puffed up lie, belying his sailor's tongue and affinity for rough language. And when an American Express commercial deified Krzyzewski during the 2005 NCAA Tournament, the coaching community had enough.

They complained about unfair recruiting advantages, and how the ad made Cameron Indoor Stadium look like the Smithsonian, and ad in which Krzyzewski says:

"I am a leader who happens to coach basketball. When they get out into the workplace, they're armed with not just a jump shot or a dribble. I want you armed for life. I want you to develop as a player. I want you to develop as a student, and I want you to develop as a human being. My life isn't about playing games. That's why my card is American Express."

The commercial was in heavy rotation during the Final Four, when coaches are prohibited from talking to potential recruits. And it seemed to be another tipping point for the image of Duke basketball.

"It wasn't just Mike, it was the players who played for him, it was everyone associated with Duke," Hill said. "When I was there, there was a little bit of a grace period. Everybody was in love with Duke. We were sort of like America's Team, and everyone was pulling for us because we had come up short so many times.

"When we won our first championship, it was like a monkey off his back. People were really excited, and somehow that's changed. It's gotten to the point where there's a lot of hate for Duke. Maybe it's because of the success. Maybe it's because there are some white players out there together on the court. But if you look at his body of work, he's been very consistent. In that way, Duke reminds me of Notre Dame football, or the Yankees in baseball, or the Cowboys in football. You either love them or you hate them, and I think we have more lovers than haters."

So, when Colangelo called and offered Krzyzewski the job, it was a project that could help both men. Colangelo would get a fresh voice, a patriot, a born leader, and a coach with great aura. Krzyzewski would get the chance to redefine his image, and a chance to make recruiting that much easier down the road.

A gold-medal performance would look great on his legacy.

"The first time I was asked about my legacy, I was surprised," Krzyzewski said. "I had never thought about that. Every year that I'm a coach, I am not who I was. I am who I am. But at some point in your life, you're going to look back. And coaching this team? How could I not do it? I mean, there's pressure and all that, but you have to do this. Even if you didn't want to do this, you'd have to do this."

During his reign at Duke, Krzyzewski had shown great resourcefulness and creativity. He created a great motivational tool, a concept known as, "The Fist." A hand has five fingers, and a basketball team has five players. Remove one finger, and the hand is severely weakened. Operate five fingers in perfect harmony, and you have a powerful instrument. He also extracted cult-like devotion from his players.

Clearly, Colangelo had chosen a coach who was more motivational than tactical in approach. College coaches simply don't scheme the way NBA men do, and at the chalkboard, Krzyzewski was no match for Popovich.

But Colangelo tapped into a powerful force. Krzyzewski has his principles and his values. Players rave at how he never seems to have an off day. But he is also pleasantly unpredictable, and always evolving. Hill still marvels at how every year seemed to bring a new Krzyzewski, and new methods.

"One time he put me in a game," Hill said. "And he said, 'For the next four minutes, do whatever you want.' Do you know what that means to a player?"

Somewhere along the line, Krzyzewski learned a lesson about leadership that occasionally evaded his mentor: If you really want power, give it away to others.

"When you're a coach or a leader or a company commander, there's something you have to remember," Krzyzewski said. "The higher up you go, the further you get from the action. As a coach, you're never on the court. So the players have to have a voice. They have to be empowered because basketball is such an instinctive game.

"In baseball, there's pitch after pitch. In football, it's play after play. In our sport, it's all going on at once. And if you empower your guys to instinctively use their talents on the court, you're going to be a lot better off than if you were standing there calling plays from the sideline every time up the court."

To these millionaire NBA superstars, Krzyzewski wasn't just any ordinary college coach. He was the guy Bryant recruited to coach the Lakers back in 2004. He was the guy who tried every trick in the book to corral Paul when the point guard was emerging at Wake Forest. To Brand, Battier and Boozer, he was an old friend. In sum, his name carried great weight and his passion was infectious.

"I like to goof around a lot," Krzyzewski said. "You jab them and let them jab you back. And then they start to feel more comfortable. They see that you're a person, and not just the central authority figure. And when they know you're on their side, they start to show their personalities.

"When I won my 800th game (at Duke), a few of them called to congratulate me. Before one of our (North) Carolina games, within a 10-minute period in the afternoon, I got a call from LeBron and Kobe, just saying good luck. I flew up to Akron and spoke (to a group) as a favor to LeBron, and then we all had a meal together, just him and his good friends."

They all saw another side to one of the most polarizing coaches in college basketball history.

"I think I can be fairly funny," Krzyzewski said. "I like to have a good time. I don't show that as much publicly. I also like to tell stories, make analogies. And some of them are a little far out. But they like it. They say, 'Coach is pretty funny.' I've heard guys being interviewed, being asked, 'What's the one thing you didn't know?' He's funny."

Together, Colangelo and Krzyzewski created the perfect working environment. Colangelo required a heavy-duty commitment, but spoke convincingly of Team USA's higher calling, and made sure the players were handled with class. And Krzyzewski knew well enough to meet the players in the middle, to mold the program around them and not try to control the show.

Krzyzewski was also furnished with a great staff. D'Antoni would handle the offense, McMillan controlled the defense, and Boeheim was the resident expert on zones. Krzyzewski also brought along three members from his own staff at Duke, namely Chris Collins, Steve Wojchiechowski and Johnny Dawkins.

That was a concession to Krzyzewski's comfort level.

"Those three were all part of a class of Duke players who never won a championship as players," said Doug Collins, Chris' father. "I'll never forget looking down at them from the stands when Duke beat Arizona in 2001. They were all hugging each other, going crazy. And then Chris sees me in the stands and points to his finger, knowing that he was going to get his ring."

For Collins, being part of this Olympic journey had extra significance. He knew the pain his father endured after the nightmare in Munich. He had a pretty good idea that Colangelo would order gold medals for everybody if Team USA won the Olympic tournament. The son wanted nothing more than to put that gold medal around his father's neck.

"It would be the greatest gift I could ever give him," Collins said.

Yet when Team USA first convened in Las Vegas in July 2006 for a two-week training camp, there was a minor setback. Bryant underwent minor knee surgery a few days earlier, and would not be playing in the World Championship in Japan.

That shouldn't have been a problem. But when Team USA rolled into the medal round, they were one of four teams with perfect 7-0 records. They were about to encounter the new world order.

When Team USA lost to Greece 101-95 in the semifinals, it was yet another sucker punch to the entire program. Credibility was stalled, momentum was lost. After all the talk of renewed commitment, the outcome was exactly the same. Even worse, the Americans would have to work again the following summer, earning an Olympic berth at a qualifying tournament in Venezuela.

"I'll never forget the scene after that game," Colangelo said. "You'll never a see a room more quiet."

During the game, Krzyzewski's image took another hit. The Greeks consistently burned the Americans with the high pick-and-roll, so much that Chris Bosh complained his team was beaten by "one play over and over again." Critics wondered why there was no coaching adjustment forthcoming.

In the post-game news conference, a somber Krzyzewski made another error. He referred to the opponents by their numbers, not their names.

"I thought No. 4 was spectacular in the first half, No. 7 was spectacular in the second half and No. 15 hit huge shots for them at the end of the clock in the second half," Krzyzewski said.

By all reports, foreign journalists were stunned. Krzyzewski had either forgotten the players' names or never bothered to learn them. They all had a lot to learn about the international game.

When the game was over, the jubilant victors danced at midcourt. Their savvy head coach received a congratulatory phone call from his country's prime minister. And back home in Greece, the Associated Press reported that "thousands gathered in the streets, waved flags and honked car horns. Traffic information screens flashed the final score, and drivers abandoned cars to join celebrating crowds."

In time, it would be the best thing that ever happened to Team USA. But at the moment, Team USA was shocked and subdued once again, left to ponder the monster they created.

CHAPTER 10

We are the World

· ·

The planet was rumbling in 1985. Mike Tyson made his professional debut. Mikhail Gorbachev took control of the Soviet Union. The Knicks pulled a longshot named Patrick Ewing out of a lottery machine. A group of transcendent musicians produced a smash charity recording called, "*We Are the World.*"

It was the year when Jerry Colangelo went where no other NBA executive had gone before.

He went behind the Iron Curtain.

He went searching for the big man who would put his Suns back in the game.

"I heard there was a guy playing in Bulgaria who was a terrific rebounder, and a big, strong guy," Colangelo said. "His name was Georgi Glouchkov. Our international guy was Dick Percudani, and he said that Georgi had torn Arvydas Sabonis apart. And remember, Sabonis was considered the greatest big man ever to play in Europe."

By this time, Colangelo was a bit desperate. It had been almost a decade since his team competed for an NBA championship. As bad as it hurt when he walked out of the Boston Garden in 1976, he assumed he would have many chances to win a title.

Nine years later, Colangelo had begun to learn the hard realities of professional sports. His Suns were coming off a 36-46 season. They had been eliminated in the first round of the playoffs for two consecutive years. They were going backwards.

Even worse, the rival Lakers had morphed into their Showtime dynasty. Suddenly, this mythical "Balkan Banger" - a player who was 6-foot-8, 235 pounds and all muscle around the basket - carried great intrigue. The Suns rolled the dice, selecting Glouchkov with the 148th pick in the 1985 NBA Draft.

Colangelo worked his contacts, setting up a meeting with the Bulgarian Sports Federation. He and Percudani flew to Munich, where they spent a night in a traditional beer hall. They took off the next morning for Sofia, Bulgaria.

"I remember expecting a gray sky, a gray landscape, gray buildings and gray people," Colangelo said. "And that's exactly what I found. Everything was kind of depressing."

On the ground in Sofia, Colangelo had one bizarre experience after another, starting with a strange woman who approached him on the street and slipped him a note. It said she had a contact at Arizona State University, and that she was trying to get out of the country. The note included her phone number.

"It was like something out of a James Bond movie," Colangelo said. "And we found out later that our hotel room was actually bugged."

That night, Colangelo and Percudani showed up at an aging government building. They walked into a conference room. They were outnumbered, 8-2.

There were two glasses in front of each table setting. One was filled with whiskey. The other was a Cola chaser. Before negotiations started, they toasted six times.

Nastrovje! Nastrovje! Nastrovje!
Nastrovje! Nastrovje! Nastrovje!

"By the time we finished our sixth shot, we were all pretty loose," Colangelo said. "So I negotiate a deal. Glouchkov wasn't going to get very much money at all. The government was shaking him down for the money. He was only getting a small stipend. But I'm getting everything I want. I'm thinking that things are going pretty good. And now it's midnight, and we need something to eat."

The party left for dinner. They headed up a mountain road. They were pulled over by military police, who shone flashlights in the faces of the visiting Americans. They reached their destination. By the time dinner was served, it was 2 a.m.

The following morning, Colangelo told Percudani that they should register with the consulate's office, in case of any mysterious disappearances. When they arrived, they found a guard outside the building, standing inside a bullet-proof enclosure.

The guard suddenly opened the door.

"Jerry Colangelo," the man said. "What are you doing here?"

Colangelo was beginning to wonder the same thing.

Later that morning, Colangelo and Percudani returned to the same government building and met with the same representatives from the Bulgarian Federation. Within moments, Colangelo was shocked to learn that everything that had happened the night before - the negotiating, the shots, the hangover - seemed to mean nothing.

"It was as if nothing had happened the night before," Colangelo said.

So the negotiating began again, with Colangelo eventually paying the Bulgarians a $100,000 transfer fee. And for a parting tax, Colangelo was charged $600 for a few phone calls he had made to the United States.

It was really a great idea. Unfortunately, it was a few years ahead of its time.

While Glouchkov became the first Eastern bloc player in the NBA, there was one small problem: He couldn't play. He became addicted to American fast food. He became the incredible shrinking import. He was a bust.

"At that time, the Bulgarian weightlifting and wrestling teams were into steroid use and other things," Colangelo said. "But that never crossed my mind with a basketball guy. And whether it was true or not, here's what happened with Georgi Glouchkov.

"He came to us with size, strength and the inability to communicate. And along the line, he just lost his strength, just like Samson with his hair cut off. We came to the conclusion that, between the pretty girls, the Snickers bars and maybe a lack of substance use, he couldn't make it in the NBA."

The Suns sent Glouchkov back home after one season. But the door was now open, and other NBA teams went looking for hidden gems.

The Trail Blazers drafted a flashy guard named Drazen Petrovic in 1986, once dubbed the "Mozart of Basketball" in his homeland. In 1987, the Warriors drafted Sarunas Marciulionis, star of the old Soviet national team. Horizons expanded, and scouts took off for the corners of the globe. And then two landmark events would forever change the future of basketball.

During the 1988 Olympics in Seoul, Team USA advanced to the semifinals against the Soviet Union. It was their first meeting since that dreadful day in Munich, 1972. It took a lot just to get these two teams back on the court.

Three years earlier, diplomats from the United States and the Soviet Union finally had agreed to meet in Indianapolis, along with International Olympic Committee chief Juan Antonio Samaranch. After trading Olympic boycotts over the previous eight years, the countries signed a pact agreeing to play nice at the Summer Games in Seoul. The competition would be whole once again, with no asterisks and no boycotts.

On the court, the Americans lost again, falling to a team that featured Sabonis, Marcuilionis, and great chemistry.

"John Thompson took a lot of heat for the team he picked, but I thought it was a pretty good team," said Dan Majerle, Team USA's leading scorer in 1988. "We were pretty successful. We just ran up against a Russian team that was pretty good and had been together forever.

"In the semifinals, David Robinson didn't have a good game, Hersey Hawkins was hurt and Danny Manning got into foul trouble. I think if we would've played them 10 times, we would've won seven of them."

A second consecutive Olympic loss to the Soviet Union could not be tolerated. It was this loss that changed the philosophy of Team USA, and four years later in Barcelona, the concept of amateurism had died overnight. In 1989, FIBA members voted 56-13 in favor of an "open competition." A star-studded team of NBA players would be the response to this minor uprising of basketball in Eastern Europe.

"Everyone took a lot of heat when we lost. I took a lot of heat," Majerle said. "My rookie year, coming into the league, that's all I heard. 'Good job bringing home the bronze.' Just brutal stuff from the fans."

The second item was of greater import. In 1989, the Berlin Wall came tumbling down, along with the fall of communist regimes in Eastern Europe. It was a new day and a new game. Marciulionis and Petrovic entered the NBA, and each made an impact. Divac was drafted by Jerry West, and together, they proved that European talent could hang in the NBA.

When Petrovic died in a car accident four years later, he had become such a fan favorite that the Nets retired his No. 3 jersey, a symbol to what might have been. He was enshrined in the Hall of Fame in 2002.

Suddenly, the NBA had a brand new accessory: the foreign-born player. Divac was almost a cartoon character, known for his animated play and his smoking habit. Meanwhile, prominent ESPN anchor Dan Patrick would always find ways to include German star Detlef Schrempf in his monologue, just to riff on the awkward sound of his surname.

But it wasn't a joke in Europe, where the seeds of opportunity were planted. And an enterprising young man named Maurizio Gherardini had already seized the moment.

Gherardini was once an exchange student, an Italian sent to live in Missouri during the mid-1970s. It was a time when the West's Lakers, Walt Frazier's Knicks and Red Auerbach's Celtics ruled the league, a time of great romanticism in the NBA. It didn't take long for him to fall in love with basketball.

When he returned to his homeland, he began organizing basketball camps and clinics. He translated important books on the game of basketball, and then distributed them to coaches throughout Europe. He organized a massive coaching clinic in his hometown of Flori, one that attracted Schrempf, Hubie Brown, Bill Walton, and some 2,000 other visitors. The revolution had begun.

"I remember when I got started, you'd have to wait in line three to four hours to get a phone line to the U.S.," Gherardini said. "And maybe you could get a movie roll of basketball highlights, if you were lucky. That's how far away the NBA once seemed. Suddenly, all of that was changing."

And then the 1992 Olympics commenced in Barcelona.

The Dream Team was legendary on many levels. They represented the finest collection of basketball talent ever assembled on one team. Team USA's top seven players were Michael Jordan, Larry Bird, Magic Johnson, Charles Barkley, Clyde Drexler, Karl Malone and Patrick Ewing. Their swagger and their stardust lit up the country of Spain.

The Dream Team averaged over 118 points a game. Their closest win was by 32 points. Their victims lined up to beg for autographs. Their head coach, Chuck Daly, never called a timeout. They were all on a mission to bludgeon the competition, and they actually exceeded the hype.

It was the perfect ego boost for American basketball, and a dazzling show for the rest of the world.

"It was something shocking," Gherardini said. "It was the first opportunity we had to touch these basketball gods. The only question was, how many points are we going to lose by today?"

It also led to dangerous assumptions.

In America, the foreign threat no longer seemed real. We had sent our best players to the Olympics, and they had trampled the competition. It was obvious. Our best were still the best, and it wasn't even close.

In other countries, the Dream Team was also placed on a pedestal. But these basketball gods were no longer ghosts, fantasies, or images on television. They were real people. The NBA no longer seemed a galaxy away.

Overseas, the brush fires of basketball became a raging inferno. Interest was at an all-time high, and teachers were blessed with captive audiences. Their game soon became a highly structured educational process. Athletes were treated and tested like students, and all that mattered was team success.

"The quality of teaching and the quality of the structure increased the quality of the player," said Gherardini, who became the highly decorated general manager of Benetton Treviso in 1992, and held the post for 14 years. "After the initial shock of the Dream Team, the international community realized the only way to have a chance against the Americans was to play team ball. The approach had to be tactical. And the love of the game was so much that our players absorbed everything."

Bryant grew up inside this changing world. He was just 6 years old when his family relocated to Italy, where Joe Bryant would play professionally for the next seven years.

"Growing up overseas, the first thing they taught me was shooting mechanics," Bryant said. "The second thing was footwork. The third was overall spacing and passing. Once I came back to the States, all I had to do was put icing on my game. I had to go between my legs, behind my back, and all that stuff. Guys were the same size, but they jumped twice as high, so you had to figure that out."

D'Antoni was also an Italian basketball legend, both as a player and a coach. He saw the international game flourish when the NBA became accessible, when satellite technology beamed NBA games all over the globe.

But the differences in approach were striking. One scout pointed to the well-rounded game of Nowitzki, who is 7 feet tall. If he grew up in America, chances are he'd play for coaches who felt intense pressure to win, even on the high school level. As a result, he'd always play on the blocks, near the basket, where his size would be an advantage, where his size would best help his team (and the coach) win.

He would never have developed skills associated with guards. He wouldn't have learned to play on the perimeter, at least not on All-Star level.

"They took all of our ideas, found the ones they liked, and turned it into their own philosophy," said Pistons scout Tony Ronzone, considered one of the top international scouts in basketball. "They don't run and jump like we do, but they're very fundamentally sound. They bring a soccer mentality to basketball, where it's more important to pass and assist than it is to score. And overseas, they promote the team, not the player.

"When I'm back in Oakland, I drive around and check out the playgrounds. And you know what I find? All the rims are bent from dunking all day long. But when I go from Russia to Uzbekistan to Serbia to Malta to Italy, the rims are perfectly straight. And they're straight because kids are out there shooting jump shots.

"We're obsessed with dunks in this country, and it's funny because you might only get four to eight dunks per game. So who's practicing the right things?"

D'Antoni agreed.

"There's a country where the first 20 minutes of warm-up, the ball doesn't touch the floor," D'Antoni said. "Everything they do for warming up is passing the ball, moving the ball. So they train to play that style of basketball. We have been a country with talented players who are capable of taking over a game. But you've got to know how to play together."

Juxtaposed to the American system, where the NCAA limits the amount of time its "student athletes" can spend with their team, and it didn't take long for the rest of the world to close the gap.

"Their kids start early," Boeheim said. "They select kids when they're young, they put them in programs, and they work them out all year long. They do a lot of conditioning, a lot of drill work, a lot of shooting drills. And then they let them play. The games are almost a reward.

"As we *can't* practice our 17-, 18-, and 19-year-old freshmen and sophomores in the summer, every kid in Lithuania, every kid in Russia, every kid in Spain is working out all summer, all fall and all spring with coaches. So, are we going to stay as good? I don't think so.

"My guys at Syracuse, we can't work them out. Most kids don't do well on their own. So my guys go to the gym for three hours a day and they accomplish nothing. The rest of the world has good athletes, and they're training year round. You tell me who has the advantage."

The changes came quick, and by the start of the 21st century, the changes were profound. Argentina won a gold medal in 2004. Spain won the World Championship in 2006. By 2008, 20 percent of the NBA was comprised of foreign-born players.

"At one point, I think Americans underestimated how much basketball could grow outside the United States," said Gherardini, who became Toronto's assistant general manager in 1996, the first European to hold a senior management position in the United States. "They probably didn't think the students could learn so much in such a short period of time. I think we exposed the weakness. We had a different interpretation of the game, and I think we caught them by surprise.

"But today, there are no more surprises. You go to Spain, Germany, France, Italy, Russia, China, and each country, each basketball nation has a player in the NBA. They have an idol. They have a point of reference."

Officially, the dethroning took 12 years. By then, American basketball had slipped to the point where its best players were tactically vulnerable. International players had become sophisticated and confident enough to play on the big stage, without fear and awe. One bad game, or one bad stretch of play, and Team USA could lose to almost anyone.

And they would. Many times.

"The international community is very proud," Gherardini said. "In Olympic competitions, they feel like they are forcing the American teams to put forth their best effort in order to beat them. That's a great feeling. They know the gap has closed. There's a different level of respect. It's the simple fact that now you have to sweat to beat us."

CHAPTER 11
His Airness
••••••••••••••••••••••••••••••••••

The first time I met Michael Jordan, I broke the code.

It was the mid-1980s. He had just lit up the Boston Celtics in a playoff series loss, averaging almost 44 points a game. A *Sports Illustrated* cover declared, "*A Star is Born.*" I was a novice reporter doing a freelance story on his newest vice, the game of golf.

I rode in a cart with him to the driving range. I lobbed him questions while he frantically warmed up, topping every other shot into the ground. When my eight minutes were up, I swallowed my pride and became a professional embarrassment.

I asked for an autograph. He signed it to a girl I was trying to impress. In my own little way, I had leveraged the greatness of Michael Jordan for personal gain.

He would grow accustomed to the feeling. No athlete ever made so much money for so many people, ranging from David Stern to Gatorade executives to teammates who grew rich surfing in his wake.

I felt so guilty that I called the tournament organizer the following day and apologized. It would never happen again.

"Happens all the time with him," the tournament director said.

For those living in Chicago, watching the ascension of Jordan in the old Chicago Stadium was a spiritual experience. It was as if a basketball deity had dropped from the sky. He was elegant, indomitable, and never once complained about his substandard contract.

When his quest was over, when time expired for the Lakers in the 1991 NBA Finals and Jordan cried with the championship trophy, my buddy and I ran screaming out of his basement, tearing into the streets like fools. We weren't alone.

In France, Tony Parker was a promising young soccer player. He saw the moment, and it changed his life.

"Watching Michael Jordan play changed everything," Parker said. "When I saw the NBA Finals with Magic Johnson, I decided to switch sports. The charisma he showed, the stuff he was doing on the court, it made me want to change."

In Brazil, Leandro Barbosa had a similar epiphany. He was at a friend's house on Friday night, and it was late. At 1 a.m., the weekly show devoted to NBA basketball came on the television.

"I saw Michael Jordan, and it was great," Barbosa said. "All the things he was doing were incredible. I knew I couldn't do anything similar, but I was drawn to it. I liked the game, and I wanted to try what Jordan was doing. And it was good that they showed this on Friday night, when we didn't have to get up (early) the next day."

In Italy, a young boy named Kobe watched Jordan's every move.

"The only teams we saw on television were the Lakers and Celtics," Bryant said. "It was Magic vs. Bird, and people loved the way they passed the ball. Then Michael came in and all this flying stuff was going on. People were in awe."

In Argentina, the same thing happened with Manu Ginobili. And in Germany, Dirk Nowitzki fell in love with Jordan's Bulls, and would awaken at 3 a.m. just to get his televised fix.

More than anyone or anything else, the man who turned basketball into gold also turned basketball into a global phenomenon.

"Michael was like Pele in soccer," said former head coach Phil Jackson, who won six NBA titles with Jordan. "He was a person that, when you watched the game, your eyes gravitated toward him. 'Wow, he's doing things I've never seen before.' He was a real magnet for the game of basketball."

In America, Jordan became the athletic ideal. He was the man who could fly, elevated even higher by the marketing power of two emerging powers, Nike and ESPN. His in-flight tricks were our nightly entertainment.

There were times when his late father, James, would stand in the basement of the old Chicago Stadium, touched by the electricity his son created, humbled by the power his son possessed. He often seemed awed that he had sired such an athlete.

There would be a price to pay down the road.

Jordan's social status spawned a generation of players who tried to imitate his offensive genius. They saw the attention Jordan earned from his dunking prowess, and spent inordinate amounts of time trying to do the same. Meanwhile, the NBA made so much money off Jordan's global popularity that it tried hard to push, package and sell a new wave of successors.

They were Ron Harper, Anfernee Hardaway, Harold Miner, Grant Hill, Jerry Stackhouse and Vince Carter.

"There was such an awareness of my offensive capabilities and what it provided the consumer that everything began being marketed that way," Jordan said. "The exposure and the marketing of Michael Jordan was everything that people wanted to see, the dunking, the scoring, the high-flying stuff. But it's not what basketball is about."

Jordan's career was a dazzling scrapbook full of game-winning heroics. There was the jumper from the wing that gave Dean Smith his first NCAA title. There was the double-clutch shot over a stupefied Craig Ehlo in Cleveland. There was the magical sequence that framed his final possession with the Bulls, right down to the classic shooter's pose.

But his true greatness was far more mundane. It occurred every day in the workout room, where Jordan's competitive temperature never waned. The man never cut corners with his game, and while some people missed that, the international community did not.

"What fascinated the public is what I did with the basketball," Jordan said. "But I learned every facet of the game. Nobody talked about my defense, but I worked at it until it became a strength. I worked on it until no one could say I didn't have an all-around game. Go back even further, and Larry Bird and Magic Johnson became extremely popular because of their versatility, because they could do many different things on the court.

"I don't like to say this, and I don't mean this in a negative way, but times have changed. We played more of a complete game in the 80s and early 90s. International players saw that. What they saw in 1992 was well-rounded players, and they saw they could advance and enhance their own games even if they didn't have the athleticism and flair."

Jordan was a ruthless competitor, compelled to dominate at everything he did. He would search for new things to motivate him, invent perceived shows of disrespect. After every season, he would find something small to perfect, until the returning player was almost flawless.

When he retired from the NBA the first time, Jordan did a most peculiar thing. He tried to play professional baseball, a move designed to honor his late father. It was a move also designed to get away from basketball while remaining in a competitive male environment. He jumped head first into a sport steeped in failure.

As a beat writer for the White Sox, I covered his every move. He'd shake his head at me as I charted each swing and miss. He worked with White Sox coaches to the point of exhaustion, and near the end of his marathon hitting sessions, he would begin to grunt with each swing. It sounded guttural and fierce, like a wounded animal.

I watched behind a chained a fence, mesmerized by this awful paradox: The world's greatest basketball player was spending his days flailing at a little white ball.

One time, I had a great idea for a story. I asked if he planned on playing any pick-up basketball over his eight weeks in spring training.

"Why?" he said. "You can't play."

Jordan didn't play games when it came to playing games. He was a demanding teammate. During his prime, he could go long stretches of NBA games without passing the ball or passing up a shot attempt. Of course, most of the shots went in, and few people dared to complain. Yet the gall was unmistakable to anyone who has played competitive basketball, who knows how uncomfortable and unsatisfying the game can be when played in the presence of a ball hog.

Jordan wasn't always popular with teammates or management. Once, he was berated by the wife of former Bulls manager Jerry Krause, who had been booed during an official ceremony at the United Center. Since Jordan often ridiculed Krause, she blamed him for turning public opinion against her husband.

Fortunately, his baseball career came to a screeching halt. During the spring of 1995, after spending one year with the Class AA Birmingham Barons, Jordan became a pawn in baseball's contentious labor battle. He was told that he had to join the White Sox as a "replacement" player, thus crossing the picket line; or he had to move his stuff out of the team's clubhouse and into the cramped minor league facility.

Jordan had enough. The next morning, he boarded his private plane, altering the flight path so it would go buzzing over the White Sox facility in Sarasota, Fla. It was a parting show of power, and magnificent to behold.

He returned to the NBA for the final 17 games of 1994-95, and then put down the hammer. In the next three years, he would win three championships; never miss a game; and lead the Bulls to the best regular season record (72-10) in the history of the NBA.

As an athlete, Jordan caused a seismic shift in the planet. He was the idol and role model for a new generation of young players. He made basketball fans out of spectators who never knew they liked the game. Yet the strongest message of his career - the inner drive needed to master all elements of basketball - was somehow diminished in his own country.

And as incoming players entered the NBA with all the sizzle but little seasoning and refinement, the audience would ultimately be disappointed.

"All the accolades I received came from playing basketball, and my personality carried it off the court," Jordan said. "The league got into a situation where it was kind of backwards. Guys would try to create a personality off the court, and then transcend it once they got on the court. It doesn't work that way. Then you had the risk of what happens when the consumers don't view them in a good light.

"There was a lot of change in the NBA after I retired. There was the innovation of hip-hop, and rap music, and some things that corporate America wasn't really ready for. Take Allen Iverson. Allen Iverson is not a bad person. He is who he is. But to try and promote him as Michael Jordan, or another persona, wasn't fair to AI. Originality is what people want. They don't want people trying to copy someone else's work. But the NBA was always trying to compare someone to someone else."

The end of Jordan's career was hard on the eyes. He kept the Wizards' bus waiting while trying to win his money back during a shooting game with teammate Richard Hamilton. He also endured a night of epic embarrassment.

During a game against the Pacers in Indiana, Jordan's Wizards were getting blown out. Jordan, 38, has just six points after three quarters. Before the final period began, Washington head coach Doug Collins told Jordan to chill out on the end of the bench for a few minutes.

"I told him if we made a run, I'd put him back in," Collins said. "If not, I told him I wasn't going to waste him."

Jordan never made it back in the game, snapping his streak of 866 games with 10 more points. It became an instant headline and talking point among the media. It was the game that served as a milepost for those looking to mark his decline.

"I told the media afterward that I didn't know about that streak," Collins said. "But I knew Michael, and that after six NBA championships, two Olympic gold medals, one NCAA championship and 10 scoring titles, four more points weren't going to be that important on his resumé."

Collins was only half right. With the six-point performance, Jordan could almost hear the snickering from those who thought he ruined his legacy by agreeing to play for Washington, for not walking away after that storybook ending to his career in Chicago.

Later that night, the somber Wizards boarded the team bus. Their head coach was sitting in the first row. And then Jordan entered the vehicle, pausing at Collins' row.

"Scoot over," he told Collins. "I want to talk to you."

Jordan looked his coach in the eye. Collins wondered what was coming next.

"Do you still think I can play?" Jordan asked.

Silence.

"Do you still think I'm any good?" Jordan asked.

Collins was stunned.

"Of course," he said. "That's why I came here. I love you. I want to help you get this Washington thing right. But if you're asking, 'Do I believe in you?,' the answer is, 'Yes.' "

Jordan paused.

"That's good, because if you're going to be my coach, you have to believe in me," Jordan said. "You did the right thing taking me out of the game tonight. But to me, the biggest question is whether you thought I could still play, and I needed to know the answer."

The plane arrived well after midnight. At the time, Jordan and Collins were both living in the same Ritz-Carlton property in Washington, D.C. And a few hours later, as Collins was sleeping, his wife headed down to the workout facility.

"She comes back and tells me that Michael was down there, lifting weights at 7 a.m., drenched in sweat," Collins said. "It was like he was preparing for the NBA championship."

In the next game against Charlotte, Jordan scored 51 points. He made 21 of 38 shots, and left the game with 3:08 remaining. He fell just short of Earl Monroe's single game scoring record (56 points).

"I went back to my office, and I tried to make sense of it all," Collins said. "I couldn't grasp how, at his age, with a bad knee, with a finger that was nearly chopped off from a cigar cutter, he could summon that kind of will."

The next game was against New Jersey two nights later, on New Year's Eve. Jordan scored on his first three touches, and during a timeout, he seemed extremely excited. He gave Collins a new game plan.

"I want the ball on the blocks," he said. "I want the game running through me. And don't take me out of the game until I tell you to. That's all I ask."

With a couple of minutes left in the game, Collins looked at his star player.

"You can get me," he said, finally allowing himself to be removed from the game.

Jordan had finished with 45 points, and later that night, Collins found out what had triggered Jordan's appetite.

"Kenyon Martin told me before the game that his back was hurting," Jordan said. "That's not something you want to tell me. You don't want to give me that kind of edge."

After his six-point performance against the Pacers, Jordan rebounded with 96 points in the following two games. And for a third encore a few nights later, Jordan recorded his 30,000th career point against the Bulls in the United Center, capping off a 29-point performance.

The milestone fell on a pair of free throws, after a foul was called on Bulls defensive ace Ron Artest. Collins still remembers Artist punching the scorer's table endlessly after the foul was called.

"What's the matter, Ron?" Collins asked.

"He's going to get his 30,000th point against me," Artest.said.

In a career rich with spectacular achievement, those three games might've been Jordan's last great act as a basketball player.

"To me, the pride he showed was unbelievable," Collins said. "Where he was at physically in that stage of his career, it was almost like Tiger Woods winning the U.S. Open on one leg."

Three years later, Jordan arrived at Colangelo's brainstorming session in Chicago. A lot had happened to the game of basketball when he was king. No one sized up the competition better than Jordan, and he knew intimately the root of all problems facing American basketball.

"Representing your country is an honor, and I felt that opportunity wasn't being given the same kind of respect it deserved," Jordan said. "When you're asked to represent your country, it's not the same as playing for an NBA brand or a college team. It's a prideful thing. It doesn't have a value on it. I felt that was being lost. I wanted to help Jerry do anything he could to get that back.

"And if I had one wish, I'd love to take my body back 15 years and play against the athletes today. They don't understand how simple the game could be compared to how they play it now. That's the competitive nature in me, but there was a reason why my career began 20 years ago as opposed to now. And these guys are going to have to figure it out."

The answer?

"College," Jordan said. "College. These kids are more focused on how to provide for their families, and rightfully so. But they're missing the golden opportunity, the chance to learn and grow and enjoy being 18, 19 and 20 years old.

"It's easy to make mistakes in college. You make them in the pros, and they come back to haunt you. But more than anything, you learn about the game. You learn about yourself. The game unfolds before your eyes. You feel connected with the history of the sport. And when you get to the NBA, you're ready to make a positive impact."

Jerry Colangelo takes over Team USA

Dwyane Wade and Carmelo Anthony hold up Team USA uniforms

Mike Krzyzewski talks strategy with Jerry Colangelo

**Carmelo Anthony, team tailor Dave Nichols
and the infamous mangled dress shirt**

Hanging out on deck, in front of the Statue of Liberty

Kobe Bryant cools off inside the boat

All dressed up for the Opening Ceremony

Assistant coaches Nate McMillan, Jim Boeheim and Mike D'Antoni

Historic tip-off against China

The coaching staff looks on

Carlos Boozer encountering the Great Wall of China

Kobe Bryant doing his thing

Carmelo Anthony attempts a reverse lay-up

LeBron James rising for a reverse dunk

Mike Krzyzewski directing traffic

Visiting the troops

Chris Paul splitting the defense

Tayshaun Prince rising up in the championship game

Chris Bosh working hard against the Spaniards

Dwyane Wade taking flight

Whooping it up on the court

LeBron James and Carmelo Anthony embrace after victory

Kobe Bryant joining the pile

Sweet revenge for three close friends

LeBron James with a surprise hug for announcer Doug Collins

LeBron James and Doug Collins celebrate together

Mike Krzyzewski, Olympic champion

Carmelo Anthony saluting from the medal stand

Victory is ours

Assistant coach Mike D'Antoni wearing a lot of gold

Chris Bosh, Dwight Howard and Kobe
Bryant celebrating on medal stand

LeBron James and Jason Kidd on the medal stand

Dwyane Wade filming the celebration

Doug Collins, with the gold medal he never
won in the 1972 Munich Olympics

At long last, Jerry Colangelo has his championship basketball team

Admiring Olympic rings at the 2009 NBA All-Star Game

The grand prize

CHAPTER 12

Heir Apparent

....

Kobe Bryant was exasperated.

"Everything that I do, it always gets back to Jordan," Bryant said.

But the voice. The speech pattern. You sound just like him.

"I don't know," he countered. "If you sat down and listened to my father, you'd probably say the same thing about him."

Silence.

"Look, I admired him growing up," Bryant said. "I watched him play for years. I've watched Mike more than any other player. But if you watched my daughter play, if you watch her run, if you watch her do something that's stressful, the first thing she does is open her mouth and stick out her tongue. From my 5-year-old to my 2-year-old, it's the first thing they do."

From the moment he entered the league, Bryant has been the closest thing the NBA has had to a true Jordan clone. He could dazzle, fly and dominate. His appetite for success was enormous. But he never won over the crowd the way Jordan did.

Jordan struggled to lift a bad Chicago team into fighting shape, and later, over the Bad Boy Pistons. Bryant won three championships in his first five seasons, and it all came too easily, too quickly. Bryant never gained proper context of what it meant to struggle, and in return, was never viewed as a sympathetic figure.

Unlike Jordan, Bryant never cried with a championship trophy. He was never cut from his high school team. And when pressed on what truly motivates him as a player, Bryant remained strangely vague, as if he was purposely avoiding the subject of supplanting Jordan.

"It's not like there's any one thing driving me," Bryant said. "With Michael, he was driven by people saying, 'You can't.' Opinions have driven him. For me, no one has ever flicked on a switch. I just feel like this is what I was born to do. I enjoy every bit of it, the game, the sound of the ball bouncing, the smell of the leather, the moment when the ball goes through the net ... just the whole thing.

"I've watched Mike more than any other player because of his height, the position he plays, and a lot of the moves he uses within the triangle offense are things I can emulate. But I also watched Jerry West and Oscar Robertson. And to compare me to him doesn't make any sense because I learned so much from him."

From the start, fans identified a major difference between these great players. They instinctively knew how much Jordan cared about winning. Bryant didn't project the same image, and his ego clashes with teammate Shaquille O'Neal made both men seem preoccupied with being the biggest basketball star in Hollywood. Being the man seemed more important than being a cog in a championship team, one of the central complaints about the post-Jordan NBA.

While O'Neal could turn bad situations into good, diffusing criticism with his goofy antics and colorful personality, Bryant wasn't as skillful in public. He came off as aloof. He was drawn into silly verbal battles with O'Neal, battles he never could win. He told Lakers head coach Phil Jackson that he was "tired of being a sidekick."

"At times the pettiness between the two of them can be unbelievably juvenile," wrote Jackson in his book, "*The Last Season*."

At one point, Jackson told Lakers general manager Mitch Kupchak that Bryant wouldn't listen to anyone.

"I've had it with this kid," Jackson wrote.

When the Lakers were dethroned by Detroit in 2004, the Pistons were celebrated for bringing a team concept and team chemistry back to basketball. Outside Los Angeles, the Shaq-Kobe dynasty was a parable to avoid, a dysfunctional team noted for what could've been more than what was.

"Early my in career, the thing that mattered most to me was playing the game, and gaining the respect of my peers," Bryant said. "The teams I was on were full of older players. I was 18. They wanted to go out somewhere, I couldn't go with them.

"People ask about team morale, and they'd say, 'Well, Kobe isn't with us.' Well, I'm 18. They're 28 or 29. And that's why people began to see me as secluded, introverted."

Eventually, Bryant would get a slice of vengeance. O'Neal was traded after the 2003-04 season, and Jackson left the big chair. While Jackson aligned himself with O'Neal during the Lakers' run, Bryant had won the big battle. Lakers owner Jerry Buss had sided with the kid, knowing it was Bryant who drove the pulse of Los Angeles basketball, not a Zen-wielding coach or an aging center with a substandard work ethic.

Bryant is a martial arts fanatic. He requires all of his security detail to be trained in the discipline. He likes that they can "mobilize a situation quickly, and not make a complete mess of things." In a better climate, he would've truly enjoyed being the last man standing in this Hollywood heavyweight smack-down.

But by then, it didn't matter. Bryant had bigger troubles.

His life bottomed out in the summer of 2003, shortly after he signed a $40 million deal with Nike. He was charged with rape, and while allegations were later dropped, the incident took its toll. McDonald's dropped him as a spokesperson. The ordeal kept him from competing in the 2004 Olympics in Athens. It pierced the facade of the NBA's golden boy.

Nike founder Phil Knight had every legal right to cut ties with Bryant. He made the decision to keep him on payroll. He was betting on short memories, and on America's penchant for forgiveness.

In the summer of 2007, Bryant began the long road back.

"Our team was all about redemption," Colangelo said. "As an individual, so was Kobe. Our story mirrored his story. That definitely appealed to him."

After losing to Greece at the 2006 World Championship, Team USA had to qualify for the 2008 Olympics. Along the way, the Americans caught a huge break. Venezuela was scheduled to be the host country for the 2007 FIBA Tournament of the Americas, but missed the deadline for a $1.5 million payment. At the time, Venezuelan President Hugo Chavez specialized in anti-American proclamations, and the climate in that country was not conducive for Colangelo's crew. It promised to be volatile, maybe even dangerous.

That was the price for losing to Greece the previous summer.

When Venezuela failed to make payment, the tournament was moved to Las Vegas, and USA Basketball executives breathed a collective sigh of relief. When a healthy Bryant took over the reigns of their basketball team, they felt even better.

Bryant was the new twist to Team USA, and he embraced his role as defensive stopper. He wowed coaches with his work ethic, often going from two-hour practices to two-hour weightlifting sessions.

Once, Chris Collins noticed that the fingertips of fellow assistant coach Johnny Dawkins had been rubbed raw. Dawkins had spent the previous night rebounding the ball and feeding passes to Bryant, victimized by of one of Bryant's whimsical nocturnal workouts.

"You have to be in the huddle to understand his intensity," D'Antoni said. "At the All-Star Game, we were up 30. He came into the huddle and said, 'OK, this is where we step on their throats.' "

Among other things, Bryant badly wanted to impress Krzyzewski, the coach he tried to recruit to the Lakers after Jackson walked away. It was as if Bryant was recreating his lost youth, the college experience he never had.

"After all these years, Kobe still doesn't knows who he is or who he's supposed to be," one veteran NBA executive said.

But Bryant would have a chance to be an American hero when the 2008 Olympics convened. He knew that much. No one was going to spoil that opportunity.

When Team USA gathered in Las Vegas, there was a new element of urgency. They had to build some momentum, and missteps were no longer an option. They had also tweaked the roster, and upon arrival, Colangelo introduced the newest addition to the team, veteran point guard Jason Kidd, who was 38-0 in his international career.

"There's only one person in this room who is unbeaten in Olympic competition," Colangelo said, pointing to Kidd.

"Yeah, and don't any of you go (bleeping) that up," Kidd said.

A new LeBron James was also emerging. The previous summer, James was not yet a man, not fully mature. More importantly, he had not yet recovered from the debacle in Athens. He wasn't the easiest player to coach.

Yet that summer in Las Vegas, the passion returned in full, and James was spectacular. He made 73 of 96 shots. He made 23 of 37 three-point shots. The addition of Bryant clearly raised the stakes for everyone.

"When I first heard that Jerry wanted a three-year commitment, I'll be honest: It was tough to make," James said. "I was kind of unsure about the whole thing at the time. I was coming off a bad experience with the Olympics in 2004. And I just wasn't ready to make that kind of (emotional) commitment. But he told me that I was going to be a huge part of this team, and by the second year, I could see he was keeping his word."

Yet Bryant was the most amazing of all.

In the team's first public scrimmage of 2007, he thrilled the audience. He dominated down the stretch, and hit the eventual game-winning shot over Tayshaun Prince with six seconds left. Then he forced James into a missing a shot in the lane as time expired. The alpha dog had marked his territory.

The Tournament of the Americas began with another exclamation point. On the first play of the opening game, Bryant immediately pressured Venezuela's Greivis Vasquez, a college player at Maryland. Bryant tipped the ball free, darted around Vasquez, dove for the ball and tipped it to a teammate to start a fast break.

Krzyzewski would replay that clip over and over for Team USA. It became the gold standard.

Team USA won 10 games in a 12-day span. They obliterated the competition, playing harder than anyone had seen a U.S. team play in years. Commissioner David Stern even dropped by to take a look, showering the new Team USA with praise.

But the most poignant moments came when Team USA played Brazil. On one possession early in the game, Bryant harassed Brazilian star Leandro Barbosa, pushing him back to mid-court and forcing the ball loose.

Bryant again dove on the floor to steal the ball. The crowd began chanting his name in unison: "Ko-be! Ko-be!"

Two years ago, Barbosa torched the Americans in the Dominican Republic. Against Bryant, he finished with four points on 1 of 7 shooting. He committed four turnovers and had no assists. After the game was over, he sought out Bryant on the floor, and did the strangest thing:

He thanked him profusely.

"I've never seen him play like that," Barbosa said. "It was like nothing I'd ever seen. It was an honor to be on the same court with him. I told him, 'Thank you. I learned so much.' "

Bryant relished in the moment, and in the attention that came with setting the tone for Team USA. The kid once labeled "uncoachable" in Los Angeles was now the perfect student, the kid bringing apples for the teacher. The rehabilitation of his image had begun.

"I really enjoy playing defense," Bryant said. "The beauty of this team is that I don't have to shoulder so much of the burden offensively. I don't have to conserve energy, and do the things I have to do during the NBA season. I can just go full bore. I can be like that lock-down NFL cornerback. And by doing that, I can inspire my teammates to do the same."

But some things wouldn't change.

In the NBA, Bryant had switched jersey numbers, from No. 8 to No. 24. That's one more than 23, the number Jordan made famous. It's also the number Bryant wore in high school, and the numerical succession is surely symbolic in Bryant's mind.

With USA Basketball, Bryant wore No. 10. That's one more than the number (9) Jordan wore in Barcelona.

"I'm flattered," Jordan said. "In a sense, I feel like this kid came out of high school and didn't have the opportunity to go to college. I went to North Carolina and learned the best about the game from the best coaches I've ever met. For him to emulate me is him getting an education from Coach (Dean) Smith.

"He could've gone to coach Smith, and learned the things that I learned. But he's looked at my game, watched my tapes, and it's influenced the way he's played basketball. He's taken the implications of my game, and put his own interpretations on it. I don't take it as an insult. I take it as an honor."

CHAPTER 13
Sweet Home Chicago
· ·

Once, Dwyane Wade stood on top of the world.

Now, he was standing on a 4-foot box. His personal trainer was giving instructions. The client couldn't believe what he was hearing.

"He told me to jump up in the air, tuck my knees, catch my legs, and then stick the landing," Wade said. "He's not telling me to jump down off this box. He's telling me to jump up, and jump as high as I can."

Wade shot a glance at his trainer, as in:

"You sure you know what you're doing here?"

Tim Grover is a renowned fitness expert who rose to prominence as Michael Jordan's personal trainer. His gym in Chicago is a Mecca for NBA players in the off-season. He had put Wade through a comprehensive strength-building program, and he knew that if Wade could land with power and control, their job was just about over.

He took the leap of faith.

He messed up the first attempt. Then Wade nailed the last two jumps. He made his trainer very happy.

"Oh my God," Wade said. "That was by far the scariest thing I've ever done."

Sometimes you sprint out of the old neighborhood and never look back. Sometimes, you come limping back home for a little help. In the spring of 2008, Wade returned to Chicago to get grounded, to get hungry, to get right.

He had come a long way just to start over.

Wade had become something of a supernova, outshining the galaxy of NBA stars for one magical playoff, and then fading away. The NBA had rarely seen anything like it.

He was only 26.

"People were counting me out," Wade said. "The way people were talking, it was like my career was already over."

Not that long ago, he was just little Dwyane, a boy who felt very comfortable playing in the shadows. He'd tag along with his family and friends to the park on Sunday mornings. They'd play basketball for hours. Afterward, they'd barbecue at someone's house, and talk about basketball.

The game brought laughter and happiness to everyone in the room, to everyone Wade knew, and it was all he ever wanted to do.

"Growing up in an impoverished area, we didn't have many things to celebrate," Wade said. "Basketball was our fellowship. We'd play all week. Then on Sundays, my dad would take us down to the lakefront, or wherever the big games were going down. We'd play with older men, college players. One day, we even saw Scottie Pippen out there."

Wade played in the shadows of his stepbrother, Demetrius McDaniel, who was two years older. Like everyone bouncing a ball in Chicago at that time, he also played in the shadows of Michael Jordan. He was a late-bloomer in high school, growing 3 inches before his junior year. He struggled with his grades, and signed to play for Marquette. He was ruled academically ineligible as a freshman.

To pass the time, he would imitate the opposing team's best player. He learned how to play from everywhere on the court.

Wade burst on the scene in 2003, his final season at Marquette. He took everything and everyone to the basket, punishing his body to score. His mother was a recovering drug addict who came out of prison just in time to see her son's final college game in Milwaukee. It was the first time she had seen him play basketball in five years.

From there, Wade sprinted up the mountain. He entered the NBA, and soon delivered one of the most scintillating Finals performances in history, averaging nearly 35 points per game. Not only was he strong enough to carry a team. Wade carried Shaq on his back, all the way to a championship.

Wade was fresh, his ascension meteoric. After the Finals, his replica jersey would be the best-selling uniform in the NBA for two years running. He had a baby face, his own sense of style, and had married his high school sweetheart. He was named as one of People Magazine's 50 Most Beautiful People. He became a top-shelf pitchman, endorsing for Gatorade, Converse and T-Mobile. He was living the good life.

And then his body gave out.

Wade was plagued by injuries for two years. He had surgery on his left knee, and then surgery on his shoulder. After recurring tendinitis in his knee, Wade underwent shock wave therapy. In March 2008, with Miami anchored in last place, former Heat coach Pat Riley simply shut down his star player.

Wade missed the final 21 games of the season. Just two years removed from their championship season, the Heat finished with a 15-67 record.

Yet Wade desperately wanted to make the Olympic team. If he didn't make the cut, it would be further proof that the new generation had moved on without him. It would be further evidence that he was never coming back, not like the old D-Wade.

He connected with Grover, who had trained Wade during pre-draft workouts. Wade had already rehabilitated his knee, and now Grover was going to restore his strength, his explosiveness, and then some. He was going to put Wade through hell.

"We had a very comprehensive approach," Grover said. "We told him how much time we needed, and what we could do for him. We could take his game to brand new heights."

Wade was ready. Or so he thought.

"The first day, he put just a little bit of weight on each side of the leg press, and I couldn't do it," Wade said. "That's how weak my left leg was. I did a couple of reps and said, 'I can't do this.'"

Grover quickly shot Wade a look of intolerance.

"He didn't have to say a word," Wade said. "That look told me, 'We're not having any of that in here. You're going to have to trust me.'"

Wade bit his lip, and for the next five weeks, he did exactly what he was told. Wade spent up to six hours in the weight room every day, under Grover's care.

"I could hear it in his voice when we first talked over the phone," Grover said. "Nothing was going to keep this kid from coming back strong. We knew what kind of athlete we were dealing with. Once we had his trust, it took off from there."

Wade's body was responding to the weight training, something he hadn't done in years.

"Forget about trying to get back and become what he once was," Grover said. "He was going to be the first guy to come back even more explosive."

At the time, Wade wasn't the only family member in the midst of a stunning transformation. His mother, Jolinda, had completely turned her life around. She also sought help, became sober, and while stuck inside a state prison, she began her own ministry.

While working with Grover, Wade bought his mother a present. It was a new church to call her own, and it opened the Sunday after Mother's Day. Shaquille O'Neal's mother and Magic Johnson's mother both attended the first service and Wade sat in the first pew, crying his eyes out.

"Everyone thinks I'm the miracle story in the family," Wade said at the time. "I think she is."

Later that spring, Colangelo called Grover. He found out that Wade was at 80 percent, but the outlook was promising.

The trainer told Colangelo not to worry, that his client was going to be ready. But Colangelo needed to see for himself. The final cuts were coming together. The Redeem Team was going small. Philosophically, the team was going to be fueled with high energy, athletic players who embraced a ball-hawking style of defense.

Bryant and James were the big dogs. The point guards were Chris Paul, Deron Williams and Jason Kidd. Chauncey Billups was out.

The power forwards were Chris Bosh, and Carlos Boozer. Stoudemire was out. The designated zone buster was Michael Redd. The designated scorer was Carmelo Anthony. The defensive specialist was Tayshaun Prince, a controversial choice over the much bigger Tyson Chandler.

The only true center on the roster was Dwight Howard, a very young player known to have a few immaturity issues.

The wild card was Wade, and with time running short, Colangelo dropped in for a visit. After watching Wade scrimmage, they had a private conversation.

"I just have to tell you that this is getting down to the time where we have to make some decisions," Colangelo told Wade. "And a lot of people are telling me that they don't think you're coming back. I want you to know that."

Wade listened intently.

"Now, I'm going to give you my perspective," Colangelo continued. "I loved you coming out of Marquette. You're a Chicago guy, so that's working in your favor. You went to Miami and you were great. You were hungry, really hungry. You played like it. You acted like it. And then you had a lot of success. Some would say too much, too fast. Then you weren't the same guy. You lost a little of that tiger in your eye."

Wade began nodding his head in agreement.

Colangelo had already been impressed that Wade holed up in a Chicago gym to state his case for Beijing. He went back home to get humble, to get back in touch with his past. It was something Colangelo could relate to, something Colangelo had often done in his own past.

"Well, I don't buy it," Colangelo said. "Because I want you on this team. And I want you to have a chip on your shoulder because if I were you, that's exactly where I'd be. I'd want to come back and prove that I was better than ever."

Colangelo finished. Wade was still nodding his head.

At the moment, Colangelo locked down a spot for Wade. The tiger was back.

CHAPTER 14
Lady Liberty
· ·

In the New York harbor, jellyfish floated on the surface like bloody phlegm. A patrol boat flanked the perimeter, armed with gunmen ready to fire. And in the main cabin of a rental yacht, Jerry Colangelo's tailor unveiled a rack of new suits.

They were beautiful.

Like a proud father, Dave Nichols had been up all night steaming and pressing the garments he created for Team USA. A fourth-generation tailor, Nichols had worked for many NBA types in the past, notably the Maloof brothers in Sacramento. He was no rookie to high-profile assignments. But this was pretty big.

His business was based in Arizona and had attracted many Suns players. Colangelo heard about him from his son, Bryan, who had raved about the quality of Nichols' work. And a new look was exactly what the elder Colangelo was looking for.

"He said he wanted the Olympic team to be totally and utterly professional," Nichols said. "Their image and how they dressed mattered, and he wanted me to take care of their dress.

"They had events coming up, public appearances. They had already done some of these things in the past, meeting with the ambassador of this, with the president of that. The team went to these events as a collection of individuals. Some wearing sweat pants, some wearing jeans, some wearing sport jackets and others wearing suits. Jerry said, 'That's just not how it's going to be.' He didn't want the team looking like a bunch of yahoos. "

He put together four options for Colangelo and his wife to examine. Together, they chose the midnight blue suit, with a light blue shirt and gorgeous blue ties. It presented a bold and powerful look, clean and classy. And despite his heavy eyes, Nichols was feeling really good about everything, unaware of the dreadful surprise awaiting on the rack.

Much had changed by the time Team USA reconvened in the summer of 2008, including some of the players. Chris Paul was now a superstar. Mike D'Antoni's celebrated career in Phoenix imploded, and he had paved his own escape to New York. Bryant had badgered his NBA team into action, criticizing management until it produced a stunning trade for Pau Gasol. Then Bryant led the Lakers to the NBA Finals, only to come up flat in his penultimate Jordan moment.

The Celtics were champions once again.

As a result, a nasty rap performance from Shaquille O'Neal was still lingering in the air, echoing like a schoolyard taunt.

"Kobe, you couldn't do it without me
Kobe, tell me how my (backside) tastes"

Depending on your perspective, O'Neal's verbal attack on Bryant was either hysterical, vile, or a combination of both. O'Neal said he was just goofing around, entertaining the crowd at a New York City nightclub. He claimed the rap lyrics were improvised on the fly, and meant no disrespect to his former teammate.

Others saw it differently. In Arizona, Maricopa County Sheriff Joe Arpaio took away the deputy badge he had given O'Neal, claiming the profanity and the use of a racial epithet was unbecoming of a law enforcement officer.

Later, Arpaio promised he'd give it back if O'Neal beat him in a free-throw shooting contest. So much for the moral indignation.

But inside the NBA fraternity, those lyrics were challenging, demeaning, embarrassing. They almost demanded a response. Bryant's focus was sorely tested, but he was determined to keep his mouth shut, and not let anything ruin his Olympic platform.

"Shaq knows what I'm about," Bryant said. "His (rapping) was for other reasons, because he thinks it's funny or because he's trying to be entertaining. We played together. He knows what I'm about. He knows what I do ... to waste that energy on a peripheral opponent makes no sense at all. I've got to win some more rings. That's my focus, staying on the hill, climbing, and bringing my teammates with me."

Bryant's non-response was further proof that he had matured over the years, that tough times had finally provided much-needed perspective. He had even reconciled with Jackson, who came back to coach the Lakers after destroying Bryant in his book.

"Who are we to judge?" Bryant said. "I think forgiveness is critical. You can't go the rest of your life holding grudges . For your own sake, to hold onto that negative energy is not good. He wanted to come back and coach our team, make amends, get us back to the top. I'm not going to hold onto something from the past."

To begin their final summer together, Team USA first met in Las Vegas, unveiling the final roster and the uniforms to be worn in Beijing. They were ultra light, designed by Nike, and purposely de-emphasized each player's last name. Colangelo was doing everything he could to keep the "I" out of Team USA.

"I've been blessed, and so have you," Colangelo said in his welcome address. "We're all here to give something back. We're all here because we care about the game that has given us so much. I appreciate the fact that you get it."

There were two unpleasant surprises forthcoming. Wade overslept, and was 25 minutes late to the first team meeting. He had to run extra for that misstep, and graciously accepted his punishment. Then Dwight Howard showed up with a slight crack in his sternum, and the media gasped.

Bryant had a broken pinkie finger. Wade had a long history of injuries. There weren't many big players on the roster. It made Team USA seem a bit fragile. Colangelo began reading the first waves of criticism about the way he constructed his team.

In private, Krzyzewski warned his team not to fall out of shape before the final training camp in late July. Then he made a vow:

"Last summer, we played beautiful, beautiful basketball," Krzyzewski told the team. "This summer, we're going to play exquisite basketball. We're going to play the best basketball anyone has ever seen on this planet."

And finally:

"Be humble. I want you, as we go forward, to think about humility. We don't have to say what we're going to do. We have to do what we're going to do. Be humble. Let's be humble. And let's win."

Entering the final year of Team USA's three-year commitment, the seeds of continuity were clearly sprouting. Deron Williams trailed Kidd everywhere, an apprentice on the heels of his mentor. James constantly acted crazy in public, just to lighten the mood and make his teammates laugh. Bryant was also making a point to be more sociable.

After gathering in Las Vegas to announce the 12-man roster, Team USA flew to New York for a whirlwind media blitz. In the front of the plane, the players started a game of dominoes. Bryant joined in, even though he had little feel for the game.

"He really doesn't know how to play dominoes, and it was going really badly," Nichols said. "I was next in line to play, and I said, 'Look, Kobe, you have to get up.' "

Bryant was stunned.

"He's looks at me like, 'You're telling Kobe Bryant to get out of the chair?' " Nichols said. "I said, 'Kobe, I'm not telling you to get up. You did it. You stink. You need to get up.' "

The room quickly filled with laughter.

"Michael Redd, Chris Bosh and Jason Kidd all put their thumbs up," Nichols said. "They backed me up. Kobe was just shaking his head. He got up, put his chair back and said, 'God, I can't believe this guy is doing this to me.' Everyone was laughing."

That game of dominoes lasted all the way to New York, where buses would shuttle the team to the opening of a temporary basketball museum in Harlem. En route, Bryant began talking freely to D'Antoni and others in his vicinity.

"There are a few games every year that I circle on the calendar," Bryant said. "And I tell Phil (Jackson), '(Bleep) the triangle and let me do what I want.' "

Clearly, Bryant was eyeing revenge against O'Neal's Suns.

"Raja (Bell) is in for a long four games," Bryant said. "He might want to sprain his ankle or something."

Kobe's mood soon brightened. It was 1:14 a.m. when the bus pulled up outside the museum. It had been raining all night, and the inclement weather had delayed their arrival by many hours. Yet soggy basketball fans still lined the streets. And as soon as Team USA began exiting the bus, it was clear who the fans favored.

"Ko-be! Ko-be!" the fans began chanting.

Inside the storefront museum was a temporary shrine to Team USA. The players were presented with gifts, including an ornate box in which to store their Olympic uniforms and medals. They marveled at some of the items on display, like shoes worn by Michael Jordan and Charles Barkley in 1992. And then they came to the back of the museum, where two giant murals hung from the wall.

One was a painting of Bryant, the other a painting of James. They were breathtaking and very expensive, commissioned just for the occasion. And if they didn't know it already, the rest of the players realized that some members of this 12-piece puzzle were a little bigger than the rest.

The following morning, Bryant hammed it up. He awoke at dawn on very little sleep, and did numerous television hits from Rockefeller Center. He indulged every whim, even playing an on-camera game of one-on-one against CNBC's Darren Rovell.

Just like Jordan, Bryant didn't require much sleep.

Later that morning, Team USA boarded a yacht for Ellis Island. They were going to take a few special pictures wearing their new suits. There was a slight problem.

Joe Johnson's shirt was mistakenly shipped to New York, even though he hadn't made the final cut. It was mistakenly labeled as the dress shirt for Carmelo Anthony.

It didn't have a chance of fitting.

"Carmelo put on his shirt, and it only went down to his forearms," Nichols said. "Everyone was laughing and hollering and screaming. They thought it was the funniest thing they'd ever seen. I said to myself, 'What am I going to do?'"

Nichols is an outgoing guy with a charismatic personality. He also has great improvisational ability. He scrambled about the room until he found a pair of scissors. And he turned a moment of failure into a memory for a lifetime.

Clutching the scissors, he told Anthony to be still, and then went Edward Scissorhands on the garment, removing the sleeves from the shirt.

"Carmelo, you don't like sleeves anyway," Nichols said. "All you want to do is show your muscles."

A smiling Anthony put on his suit jacket over his sleeveless shirt, and no one could tell the difference. The moment appealed greatly to the renegade in Anthony.

"Carmelo just loved it," Nichols said. "It was the thing that broke up the whole trip. From that point on, everyone was carrying on, laughing and joking. The whole mood got relaxed."

He's not exaggerating. The lack of sleep, the late arrival and the full schedule of events had begun taking its toll. Now, the team rallied around a moment of absurdity. They went outside, and immediately, James started to chirp.

He saw Jason Kidd leaning over the railing while holding his cell phone.

"Now J-Kidd, I know you've got some of the greatest hands in NBA history," James said. "But this is some of the greatest water in the history of the world. The last thing you want to do is hold your phone over the edge."

They joked, lobbed insults, and acted like kids.

"I feel like I'm the older brother. It's like I'm a senior in high school, and these guys are all freshmen and sophomores," Bryant said. "And Jason Kidd is like the senior in college."

Then it happened. The Statue of Liberty came into full view. The effect was sobering and exhilarating. Colangelo once gave a speech here and barely got through his words, realizing that his grandparents were processed in the same building so many years ago.

"They were the ones that made it all happen for me," Colangelo said.

Before leaving Las Vegas, Krzyzewski attempted to stoke the fires of national pride. He gathered his team around a television monitor perched on a cart. He played Marvin Gaye's infamous rendition of "*The Star Spangled Banner*." While Krzyzewski delivered many powerful messages over the final summer, that one fell a bit short.

Yet here, a real sense of patriotism filled the boat. No buttons needed pushing.

"It's my first time," Bryant said.

"Isn't it amazing? All the times we come to New York to play basketball and so many of us have never seen this," Prince said.

There would be one last comical moment as Team USA stood on the deck of the boat, gawking at the statue. Another tour boat approached to the starboard side, coming in full view of Lady Liberty. But the crowded deck of tourists were all facing in the other direction, away from their intended destination.

They were shrieking and pointing at the famous athletes on the boat next door.

"This is where our dream begins," Bryant said.

CHAPTER 15
Mike D.

· ·

The most likable coach in basketball never started a game in the NBA.

He spent most of his career in Europe, sporting an *aw shucks* demeanor culled from the hills of West Virginia. He fused two worlds of basketball into one style of play, and no one can tell him it won't work.

He is stubborn like a mule, smart like a fox. He has a bad back and a permanent smile. He hates confrontation. If basketball coaches were philosophers, he would be Ghandi.

Mike D'Antoni almost pulled it off in Phoenix. He almost created a basketball nirvana where no one clashed over egos, no one cared about defense, and basketball became furious works of art. Like Mozart on acid.

If not for Gregg Popovich and the Spurs, he could've changed the NBA forever.

"We had our chances," D'Antoni said.

On the way back from Ellis Island, two notable things happened to Team USA. Anthony disrobed, autographed his mangled dress shirt and gave it to his new favorite tailor. It would become an instant heirloom for Nichols and his family business. And an older man working on board the yacht came out of the shadows just to meet the new coach of the Knicks.

"Hey, Mike, I just wanna tell you, I loved your Suns," the man gushed. "I mean, I'm from New York and I just loved 'em. Watched 'em all the time. They were great. Just great. So much fun."

D'Antoni smiled.

"Just move over to the Knicks," the coach responded. "By now, we've got all the hiccups out of the system."

Both men laughed. Inside, D'Antoni's heart was breaking all over again.

"We were a speeding car controlled by the best point guard in the last 10 years," D'Antoni said. "It was unique. It was special. Not only did we play well and the style was good, but we had a lot of players that people liked.

"Once, I had a father tell me that he could sit down and watch basketball with his 10-year-old son, and that had never happened before. That was probably the best comment I ever heard."

Yes, people just loved D'Antoni's run-and-gun Suns, along with their rebellious mythology. They were the team that would shoot in seven seconds or less. They led with their chins, and got knocked out every time.

They began with a memorable collision of events. Colangelo had been diagnosed with prostate cancer, was unsure about his future and sensitive to his family's financial liquidity. He sold the Suns to Robert Sarver, who made his fortune in banking and real estate.

Sarver led an investment team that coughed up a whopping $401 million for the Suns, and was promptly drawn into another barrage of spending on personnel. The younger Colangelo convinced him to purchase Steve Nash and Quentin Richardson as free agents, joining Joe Johnson, Stoudemire and Marion.

That summer, the revamped Suns exploded on mixture.

"We went out to lunch at a Mexican restaurant, and Jerry asked me who I was going to start," D'Antoni said. "I started hemming and hawing. I wanted to start five small guys, but I was nervous. It never really had been done before. This was my only chance to coach, and probably my last chance if things didn't go well. And I was afraid to throw it out on the table. So I started listing options. I said Jake Voskuhl could start. I mentioned other names. And then Jerry interrupted me.

"He said, 'Why don't you start your five best guys?' I said, 'Man, that sounds good to me.' "

The breakneck Suns won 62 games that year, running opposing teams into the ground. Their swagger and style was delicious. They became the talk of the NBA, the team you had to see to believe. Midway through the season, the Suns had sprinted to a 31-4 record, and D'Antoni gathered his five starters before a game in Utah.

They all looked at each other.

"I said, 'Guys, I don't know exactly why this works, but this is something that's more than special. And we need to take care of this, and nurture this, and not let egos or anything come between us,' " D'Antoni said. "You can't put your finger on intangibles in the NBA. There's not a formula, where you add sugar here, add salt there. You just don't know what's going to happen with any group of guys. But we kept it going pretty good."

Alas, their run at a title effectively ended when Joe Johnson fractured an orbital bone in the Western Conference Semifinals. While Johnson bravely returned to action with a damaged face, the Spurs had the cushion they needed.

After one magical season, the Suns became a national brand. People all over America tuned in to watch D'Antoni unleash his players.

"I think it's the way the game is supposed to be played," Nash said. "There's a lot of movement, skill, speed, creativity and athleticism. Those are the things that make the game of basketball great."

Just as quickly, it began to fall apart.

Before the 2004-05 season, Johnson wanted $50 million for a six-year extension. The Suns wouldn't budge off their offer of $45 million, even though many implored Sarver to ante up for the durable, physical shooting guard who could play three positions, rebound and defend.

At the time, the rookie owner had already shelled out a lot of money. He felt vulnerable among the two hard-charging Colangelos, which is why he initially signed fellow Arizona alumni Steve Kerr as an advisor. He told Johnson to keep playing hard, and he would be rewarded in the end.

After the remarkable playoff run, Johnson received an offer sheet for $70 million from the Hawks. It was more than Sarver wanted to pay, and by then, Johnson wanted out. Stuck inside a bad hand, the younger Colangelo deftly played the game. He threatening to match the offer unless the Hawks agreed to a trade.

A deal was struck. In return, the Suns received the enigmatic Boris Diaw, who was wasting away on the end of the Hawks' bench. In Phoenix, Johnson was perceived as yet another player who would rather be the star of a bad team than be part of a championship brotherhood.

Then, just days after signing a $70 million contract extension, Stoudemire announced he needed microfracture surgery on his knee. The Suns' brightest star was gone for the season. It seemed to be a mortal blow.

Strangely, the team thrived in Stoudemire's absence.

As undersized underdogs, the 2005-06 Suns charmed the nation. This was D'Antoni's favorite team, one that showcased the deep bond among Diaw, Raja Bell, Steve Nash, Shawn Marion and Leandro Barbosa. They played inside D'Antoni's system with great conviction. They were all for the common good, and nobody whined about touches.

Their run at a title ended when Bell tore up his calf muscle in the Western Conference Finals against the Mavericks.

Just like the previous year, it was a horrible twist of fate. Many in the organization believed the 2005-06 Suns would've run O'Neal and the Heat off the court, had they made it to the Finals.

None of these losses primed the city of Phoenix for what occurred next.

Before Year 3 of the D'Antoni Experiment, there would be more regrettable changes. While the younger Colangelo had matured into a polished, respected general manager and had a great working relationship with D'Antoni, his days in Phoenix were numbered.

Sarver was trying to get his arms around a franchise that was becoming bloated with high salaries. He balked at giving the younger Colangelo a contract extension and a raise. While the official company line said the general manager left to pursue other opportunities, Bryan Colangelo was raised inside the Suns. He would've stayed there his entire life, if possible. He never wanted to leave. But he saw the writing on the wall, and took a job in Toronto.

D'Antoni was named general manager, with assistant David Griffin handling all the agents and administrative duties. Sarver gave his coach an additional $1 million per year. It was the worst thing that could've happened.

That summer, the Suns were desperately seeking a backup point guard for Nash. D'Antoni was already overextended, trying to serve as general manager while attending Team USA's training camp in Las Vegas. It was there where he arranged a brief meeting with free agent Marcus Banks, and signed him for $21 million. He also extended Diaw's contract for six years at $9 million annually.

Buoyed by Stoudemire's successful return, the 2006-07 Suns finished 61-21, passing the 60-win plateau for the second time in three years. Then came the infamous playoff series against the Spurs, the one that will live on forever in Phoenix lore.

In Game 1, Steve Nash banged heads with Spurs guard Tony Parker. A nasty gash opened on the side of Nash's nose. Aaron Nelson, considered one of the best trainers in the NBA, couldn't stop the bleeding. Nash missed a key chunk of action, and the Spurs stole home court advantage.

In Game 5, Robert Horry's hip check on Nash incited a melee, and both Diaw and Stoudemire left the bench. They were each suspended for Game 5. The Suns lost, and NBA Commissioner David Stern became a reviled figure in Phoenix.

Suns fans were beginning to feel cursed. They were beginning to feel angry. In June 2007, Sarver appointed Kerr to general manager, allowing D'Antoni to focus solely on coaching.

"We've had a great team for three years," Kerr said at his opening press conference. "This is not something that needs an overhaul."

D'Antoni was equally pleased.

"This is the best thing that could happen for me," D'Antoni said.

Shortly thereafter, D'Antoni left to join Team USA during the FIBA Tournament of the Americas. At a coffee shop in Las Vegas, D'Antoni made a vow. He said he was going down swinging. His Suns were going to make another run at the title the following year, and while they might fail yet again, no one was going to ruin the journey. All that mattered was the fun they would have on the way.

Rarely during his career had D'Antoni ever been so wrong.

It didn't help that a new season began with more garbage. Marion announced he wanted out of Phoenix, and that nothing could change his mind. Then during a November meeting, Kerr suggested D'Antoni feed the ball to Stoudemire a little more often.

Ka-boom.

A prosperous, happy relationship between D'Antoni and Kerr seemed like a given. Everyone assumed two intelligent, affable men would always find a way to talk things out. On the surface, Kerr's request was hardly unreasonable.

With his giant hands, soft touch and explosive leaping ability, Stoudemire was almost impossible to stop around the basket. Yet in the previous season, both Marion and Barbosa had recorded more field goal attempts, even though both had played less games than Stoudemire.

In conventional basketball wisdom, the franchise player was being underutilized.

Yet D'Antoni likes to say that the ball finds energy. His system rewards players who run and hustle all the time. It would not be customized to suit Stoudemire's personal quest, especially when Stoudemire was erratic, and often a burr in D'Antoni's backside.

More importantly, D'Antoni wasn't going to hear Kerr talk to him about offense, not after D'Antoni's teams had been filling the arena for years, and Kerr had spent much of that time at his home in San Diego.

D'Antoni blew up. The relationship fractured. Months later, when Kerr came down with the idea to trade Marion for O'Neal, D'Antoni jumped at the opportunity. He knew the old team had gone stale, and deep down, he blamed Kerr for meddling.

In an interview with the *New York Post's* Peter Vecsey, D'Antoni said the tipping point occurred when Kerr mishandled one of the team's star players, telling Marion that he wasn't the type of player worthy of maximum dollars.

Kerr was only telling the truth. He didn't know how much coddling Marion required.

"Had Shawn's contract not become an issue, I would not have done (the Shaq trade)," D'Antoni told Vecsey. "You cannot tell a player he's not as good as he thinks he is and expect no carryover of negative feelings. We needed Shawn 110 percent. That's where the unhappiness started.

"Shawn deserves blame, too. He was in a great situation and earning a great salary. At some point, you've got to understand what a great life you have. On the other hand, you've got to make him feel important. That's when we got stale. If he were happy, we wouldn't have gotten Shaq. We had a great style, and players who were perfectly compatible with it."

When the Suns' head coach gave an enthusiastic blessing for the Shaq trade, D'Antoni's supporters in the organization felt deeply disappointed. They couldn't believe he would sacrifice his style and conviction that easily. It fueled dissenters inside the organization who felt D'Antoni's lack of defense and easy practices bred soft, vulnerable teams. On the court, D'Antoni engaged in hissing contests with critical fans sitting behind the Suns' bench.

The walls were closing in.

Many mistakes had been made along the way. To combat costs, the Suns mortgaged much of their future. Before the 2007-08 season, they offered Seattle two first-round draft picks if they would just take on Kurt Thomas and his $8 million salary. They pawned away draft picks that became Rudy Fernandez, Rajon Rondo, Nate Robinson and Luol Deng.

And now, the end was near.

The final playoff series against the Spurs was easily spun into a warning label for D'Antoni's system. The Suns lost Game 1 due to horrible defensive lapses at the end. Their short rotation left them vulnerable to the Spurs' deep bench in Game 2. In Game 3, the Spurs ran one play over and over again (pick-and-roll) without D'Antoni making a single adjustment. The mood turned sour. Reports of his potential departure first surfaced in the media, and there was no vote of confidence from his superiors.

D'Antoni felt betrayed. He felt a bond had been broken. He felt too many people in the organization were undermining his authority. He knew his well of popularity in Phoenix had almost completely dried up.

Over the years, fans began to wonder about the change in ownership. Jerry Colangelo had such a good reputation among players that he always soothed bruised feelings, and always mediated the heavy arguments. He surely wouldn't have let Johnson get away, and under his watch, there's little chance that Marion's situation would've spun out of control.

Many believed the Suns would have won that elusive NBA championship, and maybe two, had Colangelo not sold the team. But he was no longer in control, and a larger question lingered:

D'Antoni's style of play was great fun. But was it destined to fail in the playoffs, when games slow down, when games get more physical, when methodical offense becomes a necessity and defense can no longer be abandoned?

On an emotional level, it's nearly impossible for D'Antoni's players to exhibit the same carefree nature in the playoffs that they show during the regular season. It's hard to shoot within seven seconds when every possession means so much. It's hard to launch three-point shots without conscience in a pressure-packed environment.

Yet the Suns had come so close. They suffered key injuries at horrible times. They were beaten by a commissioner's ruling and Tim Duncan's first successful three-point shot of the year. They were beaten because Popovich always seemed to push the right buttons against the Suns. Without fail, the cheers always ended in tears.

"I think, ultimately, we did give in a little bit to outside pressures," Nash said. "Mike tried hard to push back against all the critics, and there were a lot of them. But all the things that we couldn't do added up to 5-10 percent on a long list of things we did well. People lose sight of all the great things we did. In some ways, we tried to change because the media and fans demanded it. I'm not saying we would've won a title the way we were going. But we had a lot of fun. We had a chance. And we were very close."

Clearly, Sarver made some mistakes early in his ownership of the Suns. Most rookie owners do. He showed great humility years later, admitting that he botched the Johnson deal. He had learned a lot on the job, even if the lessons were costly. And even near the end, he knew better than most Suns fans who wanted D'Antoni on the first flight out of town.

The owner knew that D'Antoni was an asset on the court and in the community. He did not want him to leave. Sarver made a bold proposal. He offered to fire anyone in the organization whom D'Antoni felt he couldn't trust, aside from the general manager.

D'Antoni declined.

Kerr also wanted D'Antoni back, but on two conditions. He wanted him to spend more time working on defense, and he wanted his coach to expand his bench and develop players.

D'Antoni again declined. To do so would admit that his system was a failure. To do so would damage his authority among the players.

He received permission to look elsewhere. He landed a lucrative job in New York, a gig that came with his own limousine driver, but not before angering Bulls owner Jerry Reinsdorf, who recruited D'Antoni and felt misled by him.

Finally, TNT analyst Charles Barkley lit into the former Suns coach, saying D'Antoni had "no balls." Later, Barkley would say the Suns played, "sissy ball."

It had been a rough summer for a man who hates tension and confrontation.

"I was the biggest culprit," D'Antoni said. "I got to the point where it wasn't good enough if the guys didn't perform every night. Inside, it just killed us that we could never get over the hump. We didn't appreciate it the way we should've, and that applies to management, and that applies to me as a coach.

"Maybe it's natural. Maybe it was being inside a market that had never won an NBA title. Looking back, we should've held tight and kept knocking on the door. Maybe something would've turned our way. Maybe San Antonio would've gotten too old. Maybe we would've caught a few breaks."

When he showed up for Team USA duty in 2008, D'Antoni was still a bit raw, traumatized by the whole ordeal. But he wore his easy demeanor like a comfortable pair of jeans, and all the players felt comfortable around D'Antoni. They lifted his spirits immensely.

"You know what? He's actually more detailed than people think," Bryant said. "When we played against Phoenix, I used to think the players were just freelancing. But he draws all this stuff up, and he can have 10 options on one play. I've never seen an offensive mind like his. And I don't know any player on this team that wouldn't want to play for him."

In New York, this only fueled the speculation. LeBron James already loved the city and adored playing in Madison Square Garden. Playing for D'Antoni was seen as the final enticement necessary to make James sign with the Knicks as a free agent in 2010.

"They have a right to dream about it," James said. "I can't take that away from them. I loved the Garden way before I got to the NBA, and for some reason, when I get to the Garden, I always play well. So (the fans) want me to do it 41 games a year instead of two games a year. And it's been great (working with D'Antoni). He's one of the best coaches we have in the league. He's an offensive mastermind. If you like to score the basketball, he can make decent players a lot better because of his offensive scheme. He's unbelievable on the offensive end."

D'Antoni appreciated the sentiments. It was nice to hear flattering words once again. But even if D'Antoni brings a championship to New York, it will never be the same as it was in Phoenix, when his system hit the NBA like a freight train.

"And in New York, it'll never be 85 degrees in January," D'Antoni said.

CHAPTER 16
Loathing Las Vegas

· ·

With another catered breakfast in their bellies, members of Team USA shuffled into a conference room for their morning meeting at the Wynn Hotel in Las Vegas.

The lights were dim. A strange chill filled the room.

"I'm not happy with what happened yesterday," Krzyzewski announced.

The words hung in the air.

For the first time in a long time, maybe since that crushing loss to Greece in 2006, the Redeem Team was hearing something other than gushing praise. Their head coach was on the attack.

They had reported for their final training camp two weeks ago, and the team was leaving Las Vegas in less than 48 hours, off for a lengthy pre-Olympic tour of Shanghai and Macau. Reality was setting in.

"We're in a 30-day season, not a seven-month season," Krzyzewski said. "If we have a bad day, it's like having a bad week. We can't fall back into old habits. Not bad habits, old habits. We can't have a bad day. A bad day is the Greek loss. A bad day means we don't get a gold medal."

This was tricky territory for the head coach. For the past two summers, attention and cooperation of Team USA members had been off the charts. Their focus had been razor sharp. They were highly motivated, easy to coach. They had given a lot.

Yet Krzyzewski and his staff smelled problems at the previous practice. Team USA struggled in a scrimmage against a well-appointed sparring partner, a select team coached by PJ Carlesimo. During one scrimmage, Team USA prevailed only after Bryant hit a three-point shot at the buzzer.

"Let's hope that's not necessary against Argentina," an onlooker said to Bryant.

"Whatever it takes," he said, smiling.

But there was too much peripheral noise in the gym for Krzyzewski's taste, too much fooling around, too many sponsors and friends of the program loitering in the vicinity. ESPN was shooting footage for its series on the Redeem Team. Denzel Washington dropped by to check out the proceedings. It had a Hollywood feel, where endings can be scripted. It led to a practice that felt smug and lazy.

Those are words that haunted his program in the past, and Krzyzewski wanted out of this neon, nocturnal town in the worst way.

"We're not running the way we need to run," Krzyzewski said to his team. "We're not pushing the ball. I thought we weren't going to make (bleeping) excuses."

Krzyzewski's criticism was pointed. It seemed to reference something James had said at a previous team meeting. During that gathering, James stood up and delivered an impassioned pep talk to his teammates:

"During the season, when we're with our teams, how many times do we complain?" James said. "How many times do we say, 'I wish I had Chris Paul in the back court' or 'I wish I had Dwight Howard with me' or 'I wish I had Jason Kidd with me.' Well, guess what? I've got Dwight Howard. I've got Jason Kidd. Everyone is right here in this room. Everyone is here. This is what we always wanted. There are no (bleeping) excuses."

Krzyzewski responded with a simple, "Amen," and the meeting adjourned without any further comments. Colangelo was astounded at the power of the moment.

But this was a challenging time, and Krzyzewski was dealing with very accomplished, very famous basketball players, some who never went to college (Bryant, James, Howard), and some who played for programs that taught their players to dislike everything Duke basketball stands for (Paul and Bosh, Georgia Tech; Prince, Kentucky).

There was an invisible ceiling over Krzyzewski's head, places he could not go, F-bombs he could not drop. He kept his tone firm, but measured. He never made it seem like he was bigger than them. This had to be a partnership with the players, and not the typical coach-player dynamic.

"You all have friends in the entertainment industry," Krzyzewski said. "Before they sing a song, they have to rehearse it. It's the same thing with us. We've got to sing that song on a Thursday in Las Vegas or a Monday in Macau if we're going to belt out that song in front of a billion people in China. Otherwise, we've got a chance to (bleep) up that song."

Krzyzewski kept the tongue lashing to a minimum. He ended on a positive note, urging them on to a great practice.

And on the way out of the room, LeBron James began chuckling.

It was not blatant. It may have been a response to something a teammate had whispered in his ear. It may have been nothing other than James being the goof yet again.

But in this sensitive moment, it sounded inappropriate. It sounded like a guy reminding the head coach who was really in charge: namely, the players.

The same sort of thing had happened a few days earlier, when Colangelo imported a surprise visitor, and introduced him during a team meeting.

"We have a couple of special visitors here today. This is Myles Brand, president of the NCAA," Colangelo said.

"Of who?" James shouted.

"The NCAA," Brand responded.

"I missed you, man," James said, referring to his jump from high school to the NBA. "My bad."

Laughter erupted from James' peers. By then, they had grown accustomed to his audacity.

"He'll say anything to anybody at anytime," Wade said.

As the players filed out of the room for practice, the mood was tense, strange. It was an unexpected twist this late in the game, and it changed everything.

Earlier in the week, head scout Tony Ronzone floated an interesting idea to Krzyzewski. He wanted to import an officiating crew to purposely make biased calls and infuriate Team USA. He wanted that crew to call every foul imaginable on the Olympians.

The intent was to prime Team USA for the inevitable game when the officiating seemed skewed, unfair. And it would be best to blow a gasket on the officials here, in a friendly game.

The feel of the previous scrimmages changed all of that. This was not a time for stunts. And when they arrived at the high school gymnasium for their last practice in Las Vegas, the changes were obvious.

Security directed all onlookers to the far bleachers. No one could roam about the periphery of the court. At one point, Krzyzewski even barked at the audience, requesting silence for his practicing players.

Up in the bleachers, Collins was also nervous. He had been selected to give Team USA a farewell pep talk the following morning, and he desperately wanted to hit the right notes. He had a lot to say, a lot of experiences to share. He didn't want to come off as the old man walking uphill to school in the snow both ways.

But still ...

What Collins did in the waning seconds of the gold-medal game against Russia in 1972 remains one of the transcendent moments in basketball history. That was before the gold medal was snatched from his hands. The Olympics were deeply personal to Collins, just like they were for Jerry West.

The Munich Games were a hard swallow. They showcased American swimmer Mark Spitz and Soviet gymnast Olga Korbut. But they were also stained with tragedy, interrupted when 11 members of the Israeli Olympic team were taken hostage and murdered by a Palestinian terrorist group.

And when Collins gave Team USA a one-point lead with three seconds left in the gold-medal game, he thought he was going to be hero, author of the storybook ending.

Instead, he became part of the first American team to lose in men's Olympic basketball. Collins became a tragic figure, victimized by a controversial ending.

Maybe they were robbed, maybe they weren't. All that's certain is that members of the 1972 Olympic Team felt cheated in that loss to Soviet Union, and to this day, they have not accepted their silver medals.

"Every so often, we'll get the letter: Do we want our medals?" Collins said. "Some guys are starting to waver, but it doesn't matter. Kenny Davis has it in his will that even when he dies, his kids can't accept that silver medal.

"It takes a unanimous vote of 12 players to make that happen, and I don't want mine, either. So it's never going to happen."

It's not the medal that Collins cares about, anyway. It was the brotherhood he felt with his teammates who took the floor in Munich. It was the price they paid just to represent their country.

Back in 1972, coaches and administrators didn't worry about egos. Invitations weren't haggled over with agents. They invited 67 players to the Air Force Academy, divided them into eight teams, and practiced twice a day.

Collins roomed with Bobby Cremins, who would later rise to prominence as head coach at Georgia Tech. D'Antoni and Popovich also tried out for the team. But Bill Walton - the country's best player - decided not to attend. Many thought it was a protest over the conflict in Vietnam. Some thought it was to protect his creaky knees. Collins believed that Walton didn't want to endure the basketball equivalent of boot camp.

Next, they played seven games in seven days. It was not for the weak of heart. D'Antoni suffered a bad injury during one of the games, when an opponent rammed a knee into his leg.

As D'Antoni rested in bed that afternoon, the injury began to hemorrhage. D'Antoni became delirious. He began walking through the halls and banging into walls.

He would be on the shelf for the next six weeks.

"Why do you think we lost?" D'Antoni cracked.

On the final day of camp, all players were summoned into a room. The list of 12 winners was unveiled.

"I didn't get a good night's sleep for two weeks. I wanted it so bad," Collins said. "Now, there's such a sensitivity to it all. You bring in 16 NBA players, but you don't want to "cut" any of them because you don't want to hurt their egos, you don't want them to have to explain why they didn't make the team. When we played it was simple. You get cut, your ass goes home."

Collins made the team. He was sent to Hawaii for three more weeks of extensive training, usually up to six hours a day.

"It was the hardest 21 days of my life," Collins said. "We had no international experience, so our calling card was going to be defense. On the first day of practice, Coach (Hank) Iba wrote the number '50' on the board. He said, 'Do you know what that number represents? We're going to play the Russians for the gold medal, and if we hold them to 50 points, where going to be champions.' When I made those two free throws, do you know what the score was?"

It was 50-49, USA.

But here's what really haunts Collins. He felt the rush of national pride, savored what it was like to walk into an Olympic stadium and represent your country. It was the appetizer for the dinner that never arrived.

"When I heard that crowd going crazy, you could've lined up Carl Lewis, and I would've outrun him," Collins said. "That's why I get teary-eyed whenever an American wins a gold medal and gets to stand on that podium. My teammates and I didn't get that."

Finally, there was the bone-chilling omen. It had become Collins' ritual to listen to music just before the team left for the arena. Before the gold-medal game against Russia, the last song he heard was a Motown classic by Jimmy Ruffin.

It's called, "*What Becomes of the Brokenhearted?*"

"If you listen to those words, it's exactly what was getting ready to happen," Collins said.

The hairs on Collins neck were standing up once again.

Down on the court, things weren't much better than the day before. In fact, they had actually gotten worse.

At one point, James screamed at his teammates to start (bleeping) communicating on defense.

Team USA was in disarray on defense, just like Krzyzewski had warned them earlier in the week.

"These teams we're going to play will run false offense for 10-15 seconds, just to make us lose focus," Krzyzewski said. "The last six seconds of the shot clock is when they actually run their stuff. In those last six seconds, we can't give up fouls or field goals or open three-point shots.

"When I say that they expect us to disintegrate on the court, I don't mean they expect us to start calling each other jerks. They mean (us) losing focus at the end of a shot clock."

And then it happened.

The Select Team coached by Carlesimo beat Team USA in a full-court scrimmage. They were athletic, hungry and not at all intimidated.

In the previous day's scrimmage, Bulls point guard Derrick Rose - an incoming draft pick from Memphis - had been embarrassed twice by Paul, who had spotted a flaw in Rose's dribbling pattern and swiped the ball twice in succession.

Instead of gloating, Paul took the time to explain to Rose what he was doing wrong. It was a nice moment, heartwarming. Except Rose was now sticking it back in Team USA's face, controlling the game and making a series of big plays down the stretch.

The buzzer sounded and the gym went silent. Team USA had lost in a scrimmage that Krzyzewski had placed under a microscope. No one said a word, not even the coaches.

The crowd was stunned. An awkward pall hung over the gymnasium. It was as if the sparring partner had knocked out Mike Tyson.

The implications were obvious:

While undoubtedly talented, this Select team was full of young players and incoming NBA rookies. If they could take down our Olympians *after* Krzyzewski's pep talk, imagine what Argentina might do.

Luckily, there was another pep talk coming.

CHAPTER 17
Feeling Doug Collins

● ●

I t was moving day. Travel bags filled the hallway. Luggage was stacked on carts. Computers were disassembled and packed up in brown boxes.

Inside the conference room, the lights dimmed yet again. Grainy footage of a basketball game flickered on the screen:

The Americans trailed by one point with 38 seconds left. They were in furious comeback mode. The Soviets were trying to run out the clock.

It was time for Collins to become a basketball hero.

He intercepted a cross-court pass, and raced down the floor. He was fouled hard as he attempted a layup, and was sent sprawling. He got up slowly. He was a bit woozy. He felt flashes of pain in his wrist.

The players in the room were transfixed by the video. All of them knew Collins as a former player, and one of the NBA's best color commentators. Many of them had never seen this footage before.

Even if they had, no one could have known what was being said on the floor at the time.

In a haze, Collins could hear two Team USA assistants, Don Haskins and Johnny Bach, talking about a replacement shooter. Then he heard the voice of the head coach, Hank Iba.

"If Doug can walk, he's shooting them," Iba said.

Collins was electrified by the sound of those words. He walked to the free-throw line. His jersey was slightly untucked, hanging out of his shorts. His hair was floppy, his demeanor unflappable.

He bounced the ball three times, spun it into his hands, and drained the first shot.

On the blocks, Tom McMillen pumped both fists with joy.

Collins did the same thing on the next shot. He bounced the ball three times, spun it into his hands, took aim and flicked his wrists. This shot was even more pure than the last.

It was money.

The footage stopped. The lights were turned back on.

There were no unhappy endings shown to this group.

"These Olympics may come down to the biggest shot, the biggest free throws, the biggest defensive stop you need to make in your whole careers," Krzyzewski said to the team. "That's what we're getting at here."

He yielded the floor to Collins.

"I promise I won't take a long time here, guys," Collins said. "I know all your time is very valuable and I know the two rules of public speaking are to be brief and be seated."

Initially, USA Basketball considered importing Jordan for the farewell speech. They chose Collins, knowing that Jordan had been very critical of the younger generation of players, and that many young players resented the harsh words.

"For me, the (Olympics) were my coming-out party," Collins continued. "To give you a little of my background, in 1968, I was 6-feet tall and I weighed 130 pounds. I was a junior in my high school, and I did not start for my team. And four years later, I was playing for a gold medal for the United States.

"Back then, what we went through to get there and be in that position, was the hardest thing I ever went through in my entire life. I always prided myself on hard work and doing all the little extra things. But we had 67 guys try out at the Air Force Academy. We had two-a-days for seven days. We played seven games in seven days. We got up for breakfast the next day, and they announced the 12 guys. So 67 guys were sitting there in a room waiting for their name to be called, and 55 left.

"After about four days off, we went to training camp. And our training camp was in Hawaii. And we were so excited. *We were going to Hawaii!* But little did we know we'd be staying at Pearl Harbor, on the naval base, in the barracks."

The players chuckled. They knew they had spent the summer in luxury, inside the dazzling Wynn Hotel in Las Vegas. As a team, they bounced from one paradise resort to another, with catered meals and massage therapists always on duty.

"The first night there, we all slept in the same room, in cots," Collins said. "We practiced six hours a day for 21 straight days. The only afternoon we got off was my 21st birthday. Johnny Bach escorted us to the Polynesian Cultural Center and said we had a half-day to do whatever we wanted to do, but we had to get back by midnight. You got Johnny Bach, Don Haskins, Hank Iba ... you want to talk about three crusty, tough men.

"(Teammate) Mike (Bantom) will tell you, our calling card was defense. We had no international experience. We were going to be the best defensive team. We were going to come together on the defensive end. Coach Iba wrote the number "50" on the board the first day he got to practice, and said, 'Do you know what that number means?'

"We said, 'No, coach. We don't.' He said, 'We're going to play the Russians for the gold medal, and if we hold them to 50 points, we will be the champions. When I made those free throws, do you know what the score of the game was?"

The room was silent.

Everyone in the room was glued to the narrative. Kidd shouted out, "50-49."

Collins continued in stride.

"We reached our goal. We kept them under 50. We didn't know they were going to throw more time on the clock. I always said when I started coaching that we were going to play by international rules, which meant we were going to keep playing until we won."

The players laughed, but Collins grew serious.

"Our Olympic legacy, unfortunately, was to be branded as the first team ever to lose. That's what we carried with us. Thirty-six years ago, we carried the first loss ever, and that was the first time this game ever broke my heart. And the one thing you realize after it breaks your heart is how much you love it. And how you'll fight for it, and the respect you'll have for it.

"The thing I love about what you guys have done is, you've shown incredible love and respect for the game that has been so good to you. And you're making an investment. You're making an investment in a game that has given you everything in life. And this is an investment that will pay many dividends.

"Coach (Krzyzewski) said you have 30 days. I always love NBA players because they always see the finish line. They always know where the finish line is. Thirty days. The thing about this is, if you were getting ready to start an NBA season tomorrow, you'd have nine months, eight exhibition games, and 82 regular-season games. The Celtics had to play 25 playoff games. They played 107 games to win a championship. You guys have eight. That should excite you.

"I was thinking about your legacy, and your legacy is more than just a gold medal. Your legacy is that you change the face of USA Basketball forever. You can bring back the dignity and respect. Jerry Colangelo and Coach K, every single day for the last three years, they thought about this moment. Guys, I travel around all the time, I hear the questions. You think this team is going to win it? Yes, we're going to win because we have the best players, we have the best coaches, and these guys show their commitment.

"But the last 30 days will be the hardest, because this is when it counts. I think it's important that you guys recognize that you have a lot of work to do. Some of you have to get in a little better shape. For two weeks, you've got to really take advantage of this."

Collins paused. He took a deep breath.

"I was always taught there were three things in life. There are losers, there are winners, and there are champions. And there's a big difference between being a winner and being a champion. I said if I ever had the chance to write a book, nobody would probably buy it, but the name of the book would be, '*Always a Winner, but Never a Champion.*' I've never been a champion. Don't let the opportunity pass you by.

"You guys from '04 are getting a second chance. People normally don't get second chances. And you guys know what it's all about.

"Guys, this is my fifth Olympics. The referees don't treat you like stars, and Tim Duncan went crazy over there. He was getting a foul every couple of minutes. And he could never make that adjustment. The international game is about poise. It's a thinking man's game. It's eight minutes less (than an NBA game), and those possessions become vital. So you can't take those possessions off.

"This team is healthy, and this team is in shape. I know you're prepared. One thing I was concerned about was whether winning the gold medal is as important to you as it is to the international players. If it is, we won't lose. We will not lose!

"When Argentina won the gold medal in 2004, Manu (Ginobili's) interview talked about how winning the gold medal for Argentina was far greater than winning the NBA title with the Spurs. And this is what Jerry Colangelo and Coach K have done. They've planted the seeds of respect and dignity and hard work, and said they were going to get rid of this arrogance and selfishness and stuff that has permeated USA Basketball. Understand, you have to get back to work. And if we want it as much as they do, we will not lose.

"Last thing I want to share with you: It's sort of funny how things happen, but I always went to the Olympic Village and listened to music before the game. Back then, I was into Motown stuff, and the last song I heard was by Jimmy Ruffin. The name of that song was,

"*What Becomes of the Brokenhearted.*" That's the last song I heard, and that's what happened that night.

"Well, the last song I want you guys to hear is the national anthem. You heard Marvin Gaye sing it when you got started. When you get up on that medal stand, and that national anthem plays out and stuff washes over you, you will not believe the feeling. I lost out on that. But I'm going to be broadcasting that game. And I'm going to take my headset off. I'm going to put my hand over my heart ..."

Collins' voice was quivering now.

"And I'm going to say, 'Thank you.' "

He began to cry.

"Thanks," he said. "Good luck, guys."

The room erupted in applause. If Krzyzewski's voice had become a little irritating or too familiar, the 2008 Olympians felt Doug Collins. They were moved by his words. They jumped up to hug him, thank him, and slap hands with him.

It was the perfect message, and the perfect man, to reset and refocus Team USA. And as he walked out of the room, Colangelo brushed away tears from his bloodshot eyes. Howard and Kidd walked over and hugged Collins. Bosh asked Bantom for more details about the end of the gold-medal game in 1972.

Later that night, an inspired and ferocious Team USA tore through Canada. They were 1-0.

They were on their way.

CHAPTER 18

Let the Games Begin

• •

Opening night attracted the largest audience ever to watch a basketball game. The running estimate was one billion people.

The game was played before two U.S. presidents, the first lady, a former secretary of state and the foreign minister of China.

The game felt so big that members of Team USA couldn't believe the butterflies in their stomachs, or the jelly in their legs. Seating was so scarce that President George W. Bush put in his ticket request with China's President Hu Jintao at the G8 Summit in Tokyo, in the midst of serious global discussions.

The game began with a Team USA turnover.

When 7-foot-6 Yao Ming made a three-point shot a few seconds later, pumping his fist and giving China the early lead, the building gasped.

The game was sloppy. Team USA made one of its first 15 three-point attempts. Yet the atmosphere was different, benign, welcoming. As is custom during NBA games, the Chinese fans were cheering for both sides.

It became immediately clear that unless they did something really stupid, the American players would not face a hostile crowd during the Olympics.

But up in the stands, worry spread. The game was tied at 29. Colangelo was seated with Presidents George H.W. and George W. Bush. Behind Colangelo sat Henry Kissinger. As halftime neared, Colangelo began to work his way downstairs for an interview on NBC.

On his way back, he was stopped by a Chinese security guard. Colangelo pointed to his credential. He pointed to President Bush. He painted a picture of his own importance. The guard was unmoved. He would not let Colangelo pass.

Finally, Colangelo spotted Yang Jiechi, China's foreign minister, walking in his direction. Colangelo was rescued.

By the time he got back to his seat, the party had already begun.

In an instant, Team USA was flying all over the court, and the game was all but over. The game became lopsided, and what followed was a procession of windmill dunks, tomahawk dunks, reverse dunks and other frivolities that almost seemed ridiculous. China was out of energy, and it seemed like every other possession resulted in fast-break opportunities for Team USA.

The crowd loved it.

The game become so non-competitive that Kissinger fell asleep in his chair. The Chinese team was tickled to be part of history, and when Yao was lifted from the game, he again pumped his fist to the crowd, even though his team was trailing by 33 points at the time. The fans appreciated the winners, they appreciated the losers and everyone had a great time. Ming even called the night, "a treasure."

And then came the post-game press conference, when a foreign journalist pushed Krzyzewski's button:

"Coach K, there are more than 20 dunks in the game. Do you think this is kind of a show off?"

Krzyzewski was startled. It wasn't Team USA's fault that China couldn't keep up over 40 minutes, that it couldn't protect the ball or get back on defense. But there was something to the question.

As the game veered out of control, the barrage of dunks seemed almost incongruous with the humility and modesty the Americans wanted to convey.

"There was no showing off," he barked. "I mean, when you dunk ... you have to dunk, they have three 7-footers. I don't know what your definition of showing off is. To me, that's hard basketball. We played our ... we played very hard. Don't confuse hard with showing off."

Krzyzewski then glared at the reporter.

"Maybe it's a difference in our languages," Krzyzewski said. "Maybe in your language playing hard means showing off."

That exchange sounded demeaning, exactly what the Americans wanted to avoid. The exchange would be criticized by numerous American columnists who didn't appreciate the bully act. It would be the last mistake Krzyzewski would make.

Shortly afterward, another foreign journalist asked another loaded question, wondering what Krzyzewski did to "get all the players to kill their superego?"

"We have an expression in our country that when you're a really good team, you play for the name on the front of your jersey, not the name on the back of your jersey," Krzyzewski said. "Our guys are all playing for the name on the front of their jersey, and that's been easy for me."

That was certainly true.

When Team USA landed in Beijing, it was the end of a marathon journey, the end of a massive project. Colangelo had quadrupled the fundraising, from $9 million to $33 million. Team USA banked just under $5 million for two exhibition games in Macao. They had spent lavishly to make it all work, and after all the time and resources, no one was sure if it would make a difference.

For all their investments, financial and emotional, Team USA still felt vulnerable after their win over China. They hadn't shot well. They no longer made opponents fearful. In a friendly exhibition game against Australia in Shanghai, they received every break of the referee's whistle and still only won by 11 points.

That night, a reporter noted that when Australian players took the court, they pointed out their defensive assignments by number. As in, "I've got No. 5. You've got No. 10." It was a subtle show of mockery, intended for an American team that didn't always know the opponents' surnames.

Earlier in the summer, international scout Tony Ronzone had dined with FIBA officials in Greece, and basically heard the same thing.

"You guys don't play basketball," one of them said.

"What do you mean?" Ronzone countered.

"You guys don't play basketball. You play one-on-one," he said.

Ronzone gulped, but remained civil. Inside, he was steaming. He would relay the story to every player on Team USA.

"They think we're B.S.," Ronzone said. "They've heard about our new chemistry, our unselfishness, and they do not agree. They don't believe it. They don't believe in you guys. You get zero love."

That soon changed.

Before marching into the Bird's Nest for the traditional opening ceremony, Team USA waited in a staging area with the rest of the world's athletes. They spent most of their time signing autographs and posing for pictures. The atmosphere was much different than in the previous two Olympics.

While waiting for the opening ceremony in Australia eight years earlier, each delegation took turns voicing national pride, or singing the country's anthem. It was a great way to pass the time. But when the Americans began chanting, "U-S-A! U-S-A!," the building was soon filled with boos and whistles.

"Every country here, for some reason, doesn't like us," American wrestler Melvin Douglas noted at the time.

When the 2000 Olympics began, American athletes were jeered at every venue. American boxers were booed no matter whom they was fighting. At a USA-Cuba baseball game, the crowd chanted for Castro's boys in traditional Aussie style: "*Cuba, Cuba, Cuba! Oi, Oi, Oi!.*"

It didn't help when brash American swimmer Gary Hall Jr. pronounced his team would smash the Australians "like guitars."

Four years later in Athens, the anti-American sentiment was obnoxious. American athletes were warned about the hostile climate, and some journalists thought about wearing hockey jerseys in public, thus passing themselves off as Canadians. The basketball team was at the center of the vitriol, a team that lived on a luxury cruise ship.

That was a bad idea.

Yet in Beijing, a strange thing had happened. Team USA's image had already changed, and they hadn't even played a game.

"People are for us, and the support has been incredible," Colangelo said after the opening ceremony. "I'd like to believe people recognize that we're trying to do the right thing. We're saying the right things and acting accordingly. I really I can't answer why people are responding the way they are, but I'll say this:

"Our guys were on their feet for seven hours. It was hot, and once you got into the stadium, there was nothing to drink. But our guys never complained. They were terrific. And I was so proud of the way they were totally engaged with other people, with other countries."

They were off to a good start. Then Team USA began to roll through their opponents, and the games weren't even close.

They beat Angola, 97-76.

James was emerging as the backbone of the team, and his independence commanded respect. During daily interview sessions in Beijing, players were scheduled to be available for 45 minutes. Every player willingly complied except for James, who'd stretch with his headphones on, and meet the media for the final 10 minutes. No one said a word.

They beat Greece, 92-69, a most satisfying slice of vengeance.

In their last meeting, Greece ran a traditional layup line during warmups while Team USA threw down an assortment of dunks. The contrast became a metaphor, illustrating how the rest of the world focused on the important stuff.

Before their meeting in China, members of Team USA were a little more focused. They threw some heat at Greece during warmups, staring them down and delivering icy looks that said one thing:

"We had this one circled for a long time," Paul said.

Wade had become a monster all over again, more than anyone could remember. He was the first man off the Team USA bench, and he would become the best player in the tournament. He punished defenders, made shots, forced turnovers and played with a magnificent fury.

Greece had zero NBA players. But they were physical, rough and savvy. They ran over 40 pick-and-rolls in their previous win over Team USA. Now, the Americans were prepared in every way. Krzyzewski devised a great plan, gaining a personal level of atonement.

But the game turned with Wade, who disrupted Greece's offense on the perimeter, putting together a statistical line that sound like a firecracker going off in the gym: 17 points, six steals, five assists and three rebounds in 20 minutes.

"He's Flash," teammate Carlos Boozer said. "He's back. He's like a super hero. He really is. We've got him. We've got Superman (Howard). We've got King James. We have a whole comic book over here on our team."

Finally, Bryant brought great awareness to the court. Before the tournament, he asked Ronzone for tapes and scouting reports on all his potential opponents. He knew their names and he knew their tendencies. He spent inordinate time studying Greece's defensive ace, Dimitris Diamantidis.

"We're at the point now where we looking at teams differently," Bosh said. "We're telling other teams: 'We've prepped for you. We respect you. We're going to play hard.' In the past, the USA came in and said, 'We're going to win the game, it's just a matter of how.' Now, we anticipate winning, but we know we have to do this, this and this to win. We just can't show up anymore. We all have to be on the same page.

"We've shown them that we have the individuals, and now we're showing them that we have the best team. Now, it's like a double whammy."

Against Greece, Bryant and Wade combined on one of the signature plays of the Olympics. Wade sprinted down a ball that was headed out of bounds, and flung it toward the USA basket. Bryant came swooping out of the sky to dunk the ball.

Sometimes the games mean more to the fans than they do the players.

Not this one.

"When you face an opponent that doesn't really fear you, you're playing for higher stakes," Bryant said. "It was a challenge we accepted because of the way they celebrated last time they beat the United States. We knew this was going to be viewed as the first test, and we responded."

The fourth game of the Olympics was supposed to be a confrontation with Spain, the reigning FIBA world champion, and the team most equipped to beat the Americans in 2008.

It was a massacre. It represented an amazing turn of fortune.

Entering the tournament, most of the focus was on the behavior of Team USA. That kind of scrutiny came with the territory. It came with their nickname, the Redeem Team. But it was Spain's basketball team that had become a national embarrassment.

A few days earlier, the team participated in a photo shoot used for a sponsor's advertisement, which ran in a Madrid newspaper.

In the picture, all members of Spain's Olympic team are gathered at mid-court, around the depiction of a Chinese dragon. They are making their eyes look like slits, imitating an Asian facial characteristic.

"It was supposed to be funny or something," Spain center Pau Gasol said. "But never offensive."

Their ignorance was hard to fathom. Some members of Team USA couldn't believe their eyes.

"Imagine what would happen if we did that?" Paul said.

"They wouldn't let us back in the U.S.," Kidd added.

The controversy seemed to mute Spain's bravado, diminishing the collective whole. Spain was hounded into 28 turnovers, and its zone defense was no match for the hot-shooting Americans, who had 90 points after just 31 minutes.

The game was so tilted that, at one point, Kidd found himself wide open under the basket, with nothing to do but shoot.

It ruined his fantasy of a perfect Olympic tournament: all assists, no field goal attempts.

"My man LeBron gave me the ball, and I had to take the layup, even though I didn't want to shoot," Kidd said. "But then I started thinking that he wanted a triple-double. And I didn't want to be the one that could've gotten him the assist. I didn't want that."

The final score was 119-82, a blowout that further stained Spain's Olympic experience, and further enhanced the Redeem Team's reputation.

"I've seen a big improvement on their part," Gasol said. "They've taken this very seriously. I've seen their guys get hungry. They want to get back on top."

Off the court, Team USA was doing all they could to erase the image cast in Athens, where they were far removed from the Olympic Village and the Olympic spirit. They went sightseeing. They toured the Great Wall of China, and on the way down, Prince fell prey to a street vendor.

According to witnesses, he overpaid dramatically for a T-shirt that he could've had for $1 in American currency.

"He figured out all the money and the currency rates later," a team member said. "Guys were getting on him right away. 'Hey Tayshaun, you can buy my shirt for fifty bucks.' "

The players got around. For some reason, beach volleyball was a popular destination. One day, Bryant, James, Kidd and Anthony went to see Michael Phelps win the 200-meter butterfly, a race that he won with leaky goggles.

They also made an unscheduled visit to the Athletes Village, a place that Bryant called, "The Disney World of Athletes."

"It was great," Wade said. "We sat down, had some McDonald's, and Kobe and LeBron got stampeded. The rest of us just hung out and took pictures."

James couldn't believe the atmosphere in some of the houses.

"Jason, is this like college?" James said.

"Yeah," Kidd said. "I had two years of this stuff, dormitories, Ping-Pong tables, girls everywhere. It was hard to leave."

"Shoot," James said. "If I knew this, I would've gone to college for at least a year."

As usual, Bryant was the star of stars. Everywhere he went, he was mobbed. The notable exception was Australia swim coach Alan Thompson, who didn't have a clue.

"I was walking back from the meal hall," Thompson told the *Sydney Morning Herald*. "I had to go back because I left my bag there and I met this bloke.

"He said, 'How you doing?' I said, 'I'm going alright, how are you?' And he said, 'Good.' We got chatting for a while and I said, 'what do you do?'

"He said, 'I play basketball.' I said, 'My name is Alan Thompson.' And he said, 'My name is Kobe Bryant.' I had heard of him, but I didn't know what he looked like."

The story says the Australian swim team was mortified by their coach's behavior.

The U.S. swim team repaid the favor a few nights later, showing up to watch Team USA smoke Germany in the fifth game, 106-57. Afterward, Phelps visited with Team USA in the locker room, giving them a pair of souvenir goggles.

The players marveled. Howard wore the goggles over his head at the post-game press conference. During the Olympics, their egos would be tempered and their curiosities piqued by the celebrity of Phelps and Jamaican sprinter Usain Bolt.

It was good. It gave them something to match, someone to impress.

"You look at Phelps, and you see the Tiger (Woods)," Kidd said. "You see the Michael Jordan. You see the way he carries himself. He sets a world record, and 10 minutes later, he's in the pool again, setting another world record. That's the kind of focus that MJ and Tiger have."

The players were suddenly American ambassadors. They found their own Olympic spirit. They were interested in pride and sportsmanship. They were interested other athletes, supporting other disciplines.

"We realize we're not the only ones here, we're not the only show in Beijing," Wade said. "We're all living the Olympic experience."

During their pre-Olympic tour in Macau, Colangelo announced an optional team dinner at Morton's. Everyone showed up. The perfect attendance made Colangelo beam with pride. He delivered a short toast.

"I just want to toast you guys for your commitment and what you've done to this point," Colangelo said.

In Beijing, Colangelo organized another dinner. Midway through the meal, two bottles of expensive Italian wine were delivered to the table.

"It's from Mr. George," the waiter said.

Colangelo smiled. He knew President Bush and his father were in town, and surely, one of them sent up the bottle. This was a great chance to show his contacts, flex his political muscle.

"Send him up," Colangelo insisted.

Moments later, in walked George Raveling, former college coach turned Nike executive.

"Hey guys," Raveling said.

Colangelo burst out laughing.

But it was all working. And about this time, noted basketball columnist/author Adrian Wojnarowski interviewed Italian Pro League coaching legend Dan Peterson, who said the changes were the result of Colangelo's commanding influence.

"The perception (of Americans) has been simply horrible," said Peterson, a former University of Delaware coach. "Perception after 2002: The USA doesn't know how to play. Perception after 2004: The USA team has some bad people. Perception after 2006: The USA is arrogant and ignorant.

"Colangelo has been the key to me, but none of this happens without Kobe and LeBron setting the tone here. Nobody's going to rock Colangelo's boat. He's put together a tremendous nucleus of players, and he's let them know how it's going to be now.

"They're going to play defense, set a tone, and (there are) no bad guys. You don't see a superstar like LeBron coming out after six minutes pouting on the bench. What you're getting is, 'OK, it's your turn and I'll be cheering.'

"I'm doing the game on TV for Euro Sport here, and I hear someone is saying that they should've put Amaré Stoudemire on this team instead of Tayshaun Prince. I mean, are you crazy? You want a prima donna instead of a team guy like Prince who only cares about winning? I mean, just shut up. You are out of your mind. Colangelo got it right here. We're seeing that now."

Team USA pulled away from Australia in its sixth game, and rolled into the semifinals against Argentina, the 2004 Olympic champion.

The Argentina team played the game with great spirit and passion. Its leader was Manu Ginobili, who also starred for the Spurs. He played a grueling game full of creativity and contact, and his ankles often paid the price.

Entering the summer of 2008, his left ankle was in really bad shape. The Spurs were hoping he'd use the time to get better.

"I've never felt like this before, where I've been very nervous about him playing," Popovich told the Associated Press. "And if it's the same as it is now, I just don't think he should play, and I think he needs to have that opinion. I think I have to say that to him."

Ultimately, the Spurs also knew that Argentina was the defending gold medalist, and that Ginobili loved to play for his national team. They did the only thing they could.

They relented.

Just over six minutes into the semifinals against Team USA, Ginobili collapsed on the court. He had twisted his bad ankle all over again. His tournament was over. And as Ginobili writhed in pain inside the locker room, Team USA went up by as many as 21 points late in the first quarter.

Two days later, Ginobili was still hobbling. He knew he needed surgery. He knew the risk had backfired. He knew his bosses in San Antonio couldn't be happy.

But he was sorry for absolutely nothing.

"I talked to Pop. He's perfectly fine," Ginobili said. "He understands the whole situation. He understands also the way I feel about all of this. And I bet my ass that if Pop was a player, he would've done the same."

Back on the court in Beijing, the strangest thing happened. Team USA went flat. The sight of Ginobili leaving the court almost backfired. With Argentina star Luis Scola patrolling the lane, the defending champions fought back, cutting the deficit to 46-40 and aggravating the Americans with highly physical play.

And then Kidd had his moment. Few saw it coming.

When Colangelo granted Kidd's wish, the veteran intuitively knew his role would be minimal. He knew he was counted on to provide leadership and not minutes. The diminished role might be why he was so willing to part with his gold medal, which he promised to Elaine Wynn, the wife of casino owner Steve Wynn.

"Last summer, we stayed at the Wynn," Kidd said. "If felt like we stayed there a lifetime, close to three weeks. We met at a banquet, at a little cocktail dinner. She's very intelligent, she understands the game, and we just got to talking. I told her I'd make a deal with her. You can have my gold medal if we win the gold medal. She thought I was kidding.

"I said, 'No. I have one already. I don't mind. The way you've treated us here at the Wynn, it's the least I can do. And so, that's how it started. And then I talked to Steve, and he relayed a message to me this past summer before we came in.

"He said, 'Elaine is still ...

"I said, 'Hey, you don't even have to finish. It's Elaine's medal. I told her I would give it to her. So we went to dinner before we took off for here, with my mom. We're leaving, and I said, 'Look, you still have the gold medal.' She said, 'No, no, it's your mom's.' I said, 'What, my mom is going to wear two? She doesn't need to have two.' I said, 'A deal is a deal, and I'm not going to go against what I promised you.' And they're such sweet people."

The story seemed heartwarming and strange. Kidd was informed that people might think he had a gambling marker to pay off at the Wynn, like the $400,000 debt Barkley once incurred at the casino.

"I don't have any markers," Kidd cracked. "Hell, no. And the gold medal ain't worth that damn much if I had a marker. They wouldn't want the gold medal. It isn't worth the 400 that (Barkley) had to pay. He'd have to ask Phelps and everybody else for their medals, too."

Still, you'd think the Wynn's had enough gold.

"They've got gold and green and whatever else you want," he said.

Yet Kidd's sense of ownership would change. He was thrown into the mix in the overheated semifinal against Argentina, and quickly stabilized Team USA. He fit perfectly inside a rugged, volatile game. He played 16 crucial minutes. He recorded seven assists. He ran interference when Anthony started to lose his temper.

After Team USA pulled away for a 101-81 victory, Krzyzewski bounded into the locker room. He sought out Kidd, telling him it was the best game he's played all tournament.

It was precisely the moment Colangelo had anticipated when choosing Kidd over Billups, when choosing to address the potential for in-game panic. It was the moment when his former point guard in Phoenix would make a difference, and Kidd did just that.

Along the way, a fractured relationship was mended.

"When I left the Suns, it wasn't the best," Kidd said. "When you're young, you get upset easy. I thought winning 50-something games a year was cool. But with everything that transpired, it kind of worked out for both of us. They got a pretty good point guard. It took a year, but they got a pretty good point guard in Nash. And I had a great opportunity to play in New Jersey, and play in a market that's great, and we did something special there. For me to call and ask (Colangelo) for this opportunity shows you that I think everything is fine between us."

CHAPTER 19
Gold Rush

· ·

It wasn't panic. It was pressure. It lifted Jerry Colangelo out of his seat.

The game was too close, moving too fast. He needed a moment alone. He found a stairwell, and headed down to the main floor.

"I needed a little bit of a deep breath," Colangelo said. "I'm not very sociable at a game, especially when everything is on the line."

On the court, Team USA coach Mike Krzyzewski had jumped out his seat, too, calling for a timeout to counter the momentum. The crowd was giddy with anticipation. The Americans were beginning to fray.

The ball was sticking in Kobe Bryant's hand. Moments earlier, he had launched a bad three-point shot, and missed.

Spain's Pau Gasol countered with a dunk.

Next time down, Carmelo Anthony hoisted up a trey. He missed, too.

Spain's Rudy Fernandez countered with his own three-point shot, cutting Team USA's lead to 91-89.

This is exactly where the Americans didn't want to be, and exactly what they had trained for.

Already, it had been an amazing afternoon.

Twenty-four hours earlier, Team USA had convened for its final practice at Beijing Normal University. It was a day when Bryant's wife walked into the gym with a special present. It was a chef in full uniform wheeling in a birthday cake. The whole team was in on the surprise, and they all sang to the birthday boy.

Bryant had turned 30, and his daughters fed him cake.

During the Olympics, the basketball world saw a different side of Bryant. He socialized more often. He let people into his life. His unabashed enthusiasm for Team USA actually offended Lakers fans, who didn't like that their hero valued a gold medal over an NBA title.

To his credit, Bryant wouldn't back down.

"Nobody in L.A. wants to win more than me," Bryant barked. "If they want to take that as disrespectful, that's silly. Everyone in L.A. knows I'm the most competitive person ever. Nobody wants to win a championship for L.A. more than me. Nobody. But playing for your country is something entirely different."

And to a small audience of two American columnists, he spoke further about maturity, about resisting the urge to fire back after Shaq's rap song, and how he wished he had practiced such restraint in the past.

"The biggest mistake I made was coming up with a rebuttal," Bryant said. "My philosophy had always been to keep quiet and to not say anything. And by me responding, that drew me into it. If I had to do it over again, I would've just let people talk and say what they had to say ... (but) when you're young, (you say), 'Enough is enough. I'm going to say something.'"

Like many along the way, he had learned that no one wins a war of words with O'Neal.

"As I get older, I do care what people think of me," Bryant said. "I don't want them to have the wrong impression. That is important to me. I'm not too big to say that. I'm not embarrassed to say that. I care about what people think."

For a guy like Bryant, that was an amazing admission. And with that in mind, he was about to be very pleased.

On the way out of the last practice, a dense crowd of Chinese basketball fans huddled outside the fence where Team USA trained. They came prepared.

"There must've been 2,000 people out there," Ronzone said. "They all started singing, '*Happy Birthday*' to Kobe."

Every member of Team USA felt appreciated in China. That same crowd would also wait outside the fence and chant for Dwight Howard. But the unbridled love for Kobe floored all of his teammates, and it was a stark contrast to his polarizing image back home.

"People here have seen my personality more than in the States," Bryant said. "I've done (Nike) tours here. In the season, I'm in that Mamba mode. That switch is on. But during the summer, I'm kicking back, and they get to see what a smart-ass I am. They get a chance to relate to you a lot more. Half of the places you go to in the States, they're rooting against you. Here, I think they've seen more of who I am."

Yet that night, there was also a strange, hollow feeling in the air. The Redeem Team was one game away from completing a highly successful mission. After 40 years in the NBA, Colangelo was 40 minutes away from his first basketball championship. Krzyzewski had played a strong hand down the stretch, delivering two spine-tingling speeches in the last week. It was all coming together.

The American players conducted themselves without a serious misstep. The negative publicity was kept to a minimum. *Yahoo! Sports* would later report that some members of Team USA got on Bryant for walking ahead of them into the opening ceremony, separating from the pack in order to receive his own ovation.

Another time, Colangelo had to get on Anthony for drifting out of shape. The coaching staff made him do Superman drills after practice, during which Anthony was required to dunk from a standing position as often as often as possible for 60 seconds.

The last 10 seconds looked so painful that even Colangelo winced.

Finally, during their pre-Olympic tour, three members of Team USA had been captured by paparazzi entering a Macau massage parlor at 12:30 a.m. Pictures of James, Anthony and Wade entering the establishment ran in the local paper, along with a photo of one of the female "technicians." The accompanying story made little sense when translated to English, but it seemed to brand the three as bad tippers.

For a bunch of young millionaire American idols, they were practically choir boys.

"Look, these guys aren't out carousing," Colangelo said. "There's no drinkers on this team, no guys out partying. But they are also young people. With hormones."

Yet something was missing.

Team USA hadn't been challenged. The team hadn't been tested. It was all too easy. It made it seem like they had overstated the problems of playing international basketball, and that all they needed was their best players to compete.

The net effect seemed to blow apart the central thesis of the whole project. Somehow, it diminished the hours of preparation, and how hard they worked to get to this moment. It made Colangelo's approach almost seem like overkill.

There was one obstacle left. While the Spaniards were the reigning world champions, they never had to beat the Americans in 2006. Fair or not, their team had a reputation for growing tight in big games.

In Athens four years earlier, they had all the tools to beat the dysfunctional American team. When they didn't, the coach left the floor in a huff, and was promptly pulled inside a room, forced to explain himself to the king and queen.

In 2008, Spain fielded a team full of flashy, versatile players. Gasol was a nimble big man who could run the floor. His brother, Marc, had made great improvements as a post player. Fernandez had great skill and leaping ability. Jose Calderon played for the Raptors. And 17-year-old point guard Ricky Rubio was said to be the reincarnation of Pistol Pete Maravich.

But their artistic, up-tempo game was demolished by the Americans in their first Beijing encounter, where Spain lost by 37 points. Rubio looked like a boy among men, all hype and no impact. Calderon was subsequently injured, and couldn't play in the gold-medal match. Not many gave Spain, or it's approach, much of a chance.

"You have to play ugly," Argentina's Luis Scola said. "If you try to play, 'Showtime' the way they play, if you try to throw the ball up for alley-oops, they're going to get it. They jump higher, they run faster, they're stronger. You've got to play ugly. Physical. You've got to make them uncomfortable. That's the only way."

The gold-medal game belied all of that. Early on, Rubio had made a string of flashy plays, changing the complexion of the game. He was far too quick for Kidd, who soon had a seat on the bench. Bryant and James each picked their second personal fouls before the first quarter was over, and Team USA was under assault.

Bosh replaced Howard, and would take most of his minutes. This was a recurring theme during the tournament. Bosh was athletic, long and strong. He was smart, driven and energetic. The team was far more potent with him in the game, and everyone knew it.

Then Wade and Deron Williams entered the game, and played like hungry jackals.

Williams is extremely strong and loves to play physical. He immediately threw his weight into Rubio, thus throwing him out of rhythm, off his game. Wade showed off his new power, and in 13:10 of playing time in the first half, his statistical line was staggering.

Wade had collected 21 points, four steals, and made three three-point shots. But the Spaniards never quit.

The gold-medal game wasn't a made-for-television event in the United States, not a consumer spectacle like the Super Bowl. Tip-off occurred at 2:30 a.m. Eastern Standard Time, and by the time most Americans watched a replay of the game, they were already aware of the outcome.

While the magnitude of the game has been a frequent topic of discussion, the beauty of the game has been overlooked and underappreciated. After 20 minutes of basketball that featured zero television timeouts, the two teams had scored 130 points. Spain played 11 men in the first half, and the only Americans not to play were Carlos Boozer and Michael Redd.

Both teams were running hard, cutting hard, and absorbing contact. The shot-making was stupendous. When the first half ended, those in the gymnasium knew that something had to give, namely the quality of play.

It didn't.

The second half was even better. The Americans were getting the test they needed, and Spain was starting to play with swagger. They sensed a great chance to pull of the upset. With 170 points on the scoreboard, only one basket separated these two teams.

As Colangelo barreled down the stairs, Krzyzewski gathered his players. Inside the huddle, Bryant knew what he was going to do.

He was going to shoot.

Out of the timeout, he made a great play off the dribble, sinking an acrobatic shot in the lane. Then he fed Howard for a dunk. Then he countered a three-point shot from Fernandez with a three-point shot of his own.

The lead was safe once again. Team USA had fended off one charge. Next.

Trailing 103-92 with just over five minutes remaining, Fernandez drove the lane with Howard on his left side. Fernandez is 6-foot-6. He is 5 inches shorter than Howard, and at least 80 pounds lighter. Yet he soared for a tomahawk dunk over the Magic star, drawing a foul in the process.

Ironically, Fernandez's dunk came over the reigning NBA slam dunk champion. And when a player from Team USA gets poster-ized by a foreign competitor, you know the game of basketball has come full circle.

"For me, it was great," Fernandez said six months later. "For me, it (brought) respect, doing it against Howard. Still, this (dunk) is what everyone (wants to) talk to me about."

But Bryant had yet another moment. Team USA led 104-99 when Wade drove the lane, collapsed the defense, and fired the ball back outside to a wide-open Bryant. He hesitated for a moment, allowing Fernandez to recover defensively.

Undaunted, he drained a deep three-point shot in the face of his opponent.

Better yet, Bryant also drew contact and a whistle, fouling Fernandez out of the game. It was a four-point, game-changing play, and when the shot went through the net, Bryant stood motionless. He looked at a section of the crowd that had been cheering hard for Spain.

He put a finger to his lips.

Kobe, you can't do it without me?

That shhhhh might've just as well been for Shaq.

Down to a few desperation punches, Spain cut the deficit to four points one last time. Fittingly, it was Wade who delivered the final blow, hitting another huge three-point shot.

This time, it was really over. Boozer and Redd checked into the game with 26.1 seconds left, as Krzyzewski worked everyone into the box score. Then the horn sounded, and Bruce Springsteen's *"Born in the USA"* blared over the public address system.

Krzyzewski kissed Colangelo on the cheek. James led a few other players to the broadcast table, bringing their medals directly to Collins and draping them over his neck.

"The game was unbelievable," James said. "Every possession counted ... it will probably go down in history as one of the greatest Olympic games ever."

Over the previous two weeks, an interesting debate had been sparked in Beijing. Was the Redeem Team actually better than the Dream Team?

Some said the 2008 team was quicker, younger, more athletic. Proponents of the Redeem Team pointed out that the competition was much weaker in 1992, that Magic Johnson had already retired from the NBA and that Larry Bird was 35 and on his way out, succumbing to a chronic back injury. He didn't play that much in those Olympics.

Others said any team with that kind of pedigree, including a rabid Jordan in his prime, would never be conquered.

By nightfall in Beijing, it didn't matter. The game had instantly stamped the legacy of the Redeem Team. Under stifling pressure, they didn't revert to bad habits. They didn't crack. They didn't struggle with teamwork and ball movement. They didn't resort to their superior individual skills.

"Had we not been together for three years, we might've cracked," Colangelo said. "Individuals might've gone one-on-one. That would've been the tendency. But I think the continuity paid off."

The game was validation for Colangelo and Krzyzewski, the two men who plotted the course. It was the comeback party for Wade, vengeance for Anthony and James, and the sweetest moment of Bryant's life.

As he finished off his on-court interviews, a song by Lupe Fiasco played over the loudspeakers. The lyrics were fitting, almost ethereal.

If you are what you say you are, a superstar...
Then have no fear, the time is here...

Bryant bounced to the song as he ran into the locker room. He was the last person off the court. His smile seemed to stretch all the way to his ears.

Back home, the game cleansed the perception of NBA players. Team USA had respected the opponent and the game. They showed heavy mettle. When it came time to close out a gold- medal performance, they acted like champions.

They answered every big moment with a bolder stroke of their own. They made 60 percent of their shots in the biggest game of their lives.

"I think this is a testament to the system that Mr. Colangelo put in place," Bryant said. "Because what you saw today was a team. Everybody wants to talk about the NBA players being selfish, being arrogant, being individuals. But what you saw today was a team bonding together, facing adversity and coming out of here with a big win."

And then the strangest thing happened.

While Team USA celebrated on the court, Spain's team huddled together, and did a little dance. They were smiling and bonding and acting like they had won the game.

"Back home, they were extremely proud of us," Gasol said six months later. "They thought we deserved the gold. A lot of people said, 'Don't worry. It's not a silver medal. It's a gold medal to us.' So we were really happy."

It was all too good to be true. The championship match brought redemption to both teams. Everybody won. Team Spain regained its dignity. Team USA returned the gold to America. Basketball had truly become the world's game, and it never looked better.

"What I remember most is how good we had to play to beat them," D'Antoni said. "We played by far our best game, we did it in the gold-medal game, and it was still close at the end. It validated everything we went through in the last three years, getting the team to the point where they understood they needed all of that.

"We saw the hardest game we could imagine. The players were prepared for an unbelievable game from the opponent. If Spain played their normal game, we would've beat the (expletive) out of them."

The Olympics were just about over.

Except nothing is really over with Team USA until James says it's over.

CHAPTER 20
King James
....

Every member of Team USA showed up for the post-game press conference. There were only six chairs available.

Kidd claimed one out of seniority. Bryant and James saddled up next to Krzyzewski. Anthony took a seat. Craig Miller, director of media relations for USA Basketball, implored Colangelo to join all of them all on stage.

Most of the players stood at the back of the podium. They were all draped in American flags.

Krzyzewski looked at James.

"You may not want to sit next to me," he said. "I smell like (expletive)."

The media laughed. The microphones were hot, the players too giddy to care. And after some opening remarks, the first question caused a stir, just like it had after the opening game against China:

Reporter: "You guys have too many scorers on the team and ..."

Krzyzewski: "Who said?"

Reporter: "I read it in the newspaper in Sweden."

Krzyzewski: "Don't believe everything you read in the paper. I said that?"

James: "Gossip mags don't count."

Krzyzewski: "Are you with the Enquirer?"

Reporter: "No, Swedish TV."

Krzyzewski: "First of all, I never said that."

Reporter: "I didn't say you said it. I said I read it in Swedish newspapers."

James: "You've got good massages, right?"

Reporter: "Not from me, though."

James, smiling: "No, I didn't say you."

By now, the room was almost hysterical with laughter.

The exchange was fascinating, illustrating Krzyzewski's deep concern about image. In trying so hard not to be disrespectful, he would occasionally make things worse. Meanwhile, James interrupted another conversation with an outrageous line. This one seemed to be shaped by his experience with the paparazzi in Macau.

But it wasn't his words that mattered. It was the command in his voice, the sense of authority, the impermeable self-confidence. For a man-child who was only 23, James' presence was striking, almost other-worldly.

At one point, the world seemed to collude against James, blessing him with riches, cursing him with unprecedented hype, and turning him into a freak show.

He was on the cover of *Sports Illustrated* and *ESPN: The Magazine* before his senior year of high school, and James was a television star before graduating high school. Some of his prep games were televised by ESPN2. The first one drew a 1.97 rating (1.67 million homes), and was the highest-rated show the channel had aired in more than two years. Some of his games were available on regional pay-per-view.

He was such a draw that his team moved its home games to the University of Akron, playing inside a 5,900-seat arena.

His team would also travel all over the country to play games, from New Jersey to Los Angeles. Once, James sold out Pauley Pavilion on the campus of UCLA. In return, the competing team received hotel, air fare and limousines to the arena and who knows what else. They were honored at a luncheon at the Lawry's in Beverly Hills.

A story in *The Los Angeles Times* before the game told of an incident when James' handlers were approached by an event photographer.

"I need two minutes with him," the photographer said.

"You got one," James snapped.

And then James sat patiently, taking countless pictures and bringing his teammates into many of the poses. He just need to establish who was in control.

Later, there would be trouble. Although they lived in an impoverished area, James' mother bought James a customized Hummer for his 18th birthday, arranging a loan against future earnings. The cost of the vehicle was reportedly $50,000 to $80,000. Then James accepted two expensive retro jerseys - Gale Sayers, Wes Unseld - that nearly cost him his high school eligibility.

James became the poster boy for corrupted youth, for the end of innocence in high school basketball. Outrage filled the airwaves.

The hypocrisy was striking, laughable, shameful. Adults had been exploiting James for years, making money off his reputation and his unique talent. And now they were condemning him for wanting in on the game.

But a funny thing happened along the way. James met the hype and then some. He was only 18 when he played his first NBA game, but produced 25 points, nine assists and six rebounds.

It was by far the most impressive debut performance from a kid who had jumped to the NBA straight from high school: Stoudemire (10 points), Bryant (no points), Jonathan Bender (10), Kevin Garnett (eight), Jermaine O'Neal (two), Kwame Brown (two), Eddy Curry (two), Tyson Chandler (one) and Tracy McGrady (no points).

Just like Jordan, James eventually lifted his team past a rugged championship team from Detroit, almost singlehandedly eliminating the Pistons in the 2007 Eastern Conference Finals. His signature performance came in a double-overtime victory when

James produced 48 points, closing out the game by scoring the Cavaliers' final 25 points.

Then James was swallowed up by the savvy Spurs, swept in his first NBA Finals.

Nevertheless, James was an instant impact player in the NBA. He's a giant man with an unprecedented combination of speed, agility and power. His aura and the swooping dunks hit the NBA just like Dr. J so many years ago.

"LeBron is like a bull in a china shop," Julius Erving said. "I don't even know if he knows how good he is. To look at a guy coming full speed at 270 pounds, that's like Shaq being a point guard. He's like, 'All you little boys have to get out of the way.' "

Erving and James have a lot in common. Both exude cool. Both have superstar musician friends. And just like Erving once did, James immerses himself in music before games.

"My favorite musician was Grover Washington Jr., because he was a friend and he composed a song for me surrounding basketball (called), 'Let it Flow'," Erving said. "But for pre-game music, it was Marvin Gaye and Earth, Wind & Fire.

"Certain games, I was in a Marvin Gaye mode. 'Let's Get it On' or whatever. But in other games, like when we played Boston or New York, playing your rivals, it was Earth, Wind & Fire all the way. Shining star, no matter who you are."

Clearly ahead of his time, Erving brought basketball to a new elevation, literally and figuratively. He legitimized the ABA and then electrified the NBA. And while he never played for his country, he was no stranger to international basketball.

"I probably played more international basketball than any player of my era," Erving said. "I used to travel abroad with Converse and Spalding, put on clinics, play games, do retail setups, try to sell Converse and Spalding in Asia, South America and Europe. I did that all 16 years of my career. So a lot of my identity outside the U.S. came from being a peddler of sneakers and balls.

"I missed the Olympics. I was too young for '68 and was already a pro in '72. But when I go back as a citizen of the world, I still have recognition and respect, and that's nice."

Erving also spawned a new generation of players. One of them was David Thompson, known for his vertical leap. His nickname - Skywalker - said it all.

"I was the first one who brought in the term vertical leap," Thompson said. "When I played in college, you couldn't dunk the basketball. You had to catch the ball and drop it into the basket. So my first year in the NBA, I went baseline, cradled the ball, dunked over Bill Walton and shattered the backboard. That was pretty nasty. But we were all paying tribute to Dr. J."

Erving was also a member of the old school, and not easily impressed. Before the Lakers acquired Gasol and made a run for the title in 2008, he criticized Bryant on a Los Angeles radio station, saying it "would be pretty easy to replace him because he's left a lot of work undone."

But Erving saw a lot of changes in Bryant after the 2008 Olympics. And he saw a growing monster in James, someone who could rock the NBA the way he had many years ago.

Dr. J. was beginning to love the NBA all over again.

"I think Kobe and LeBron are leading the charge," Erving said. "And I think what you have is a torch-bearing situation. Kobe has it now. He has the experience, and there's no substitute for that. Kobe has the entire package, and I think LeBron would admit that.

"Well, maybe because of their egos, neither one of them would admit it. But that's part of it. Don't give any quarter to anybody who can put you at a disadvantage. So Kobe's got the torch now, and LeBron is next in line."

It may not take long, and mostly, it's a matter of where.

While James shares the ball willingly, he does everything on his own terms. While it's customary for NBA franchises to cater to their star players, James and his impending free agency has had the Cavaliers paralyzed with fear, bending to his every whim.

The leverage made James more powerful than ever. He isn't afraid to wear a Yankees hat while living in Cleveland. He isn't afraid to gush about Madison Square Garden. The strength he projects makes him a natural leader.

He doesn't make mistakes. Not usually. But once, during a televised playoff game, he went tumbling into the stands with the Celtics' Paul Pierce. It was a rough game and a hard foul, and it just so happened that LeBron's mother, Gloria, was sitting nearby.

Her maternal instincts kicked in. She jumped up to defend her baby and began wagging her finger and jawing at Pierce. James then told his mother to "sit yo (backside) down."

She complied. Afterward, James showed great remorse and great wit.

"I told her to sit down with some language I shouldn't have used," James told reporters. "Thank God it wasn't Mother's Day."

James also has a close team guarding his back. During the final training camp in 2008, he was playing blackjack at the Wynn when a nearby bar patron noticed the famous player. The fan took a few photos from his camera phone, just for posterity. And within seconds, James' handlers alerted security, had the phone confiscated and the pictures removed.

The fan had his feelings bruised, but pictures of James gambling in Las Vegas were not going to end up on the Internet.

In short, James is a genetic marvel. Every member of the Team USA hierarchy couldn't believe the evolution of his game, his leadership, and his voice over the span of three years. And if you ever saw him change his shirt in the locker room, you'd see a tattoo that stretches across his back: CHOSEN 1.

"I think when it's all said and done, he's going to be the greatest (player) ever," D'Antoni said.

Yet after the gold-medal game in Beijing, James was getting antsy. He wanted to move on, and move out. He began to fidget through the interviews:

Krzyzewski: "Look, this was easy. All these guys committed to Jerry Colangelo three years ago, and they said they wanted to be part of the team. Jerry said, 'We're going to have one collective ego. But we want you to bring all your egos because that's how you get better. We have not had one second of problem as a coaching staff with our team. It's been the greatest experience of my life, and the lives of the other coaches."

Colangelo: "I think the guys forgot this is a six-year commitment. Seriously, we're going to celebrate, and we're going to talk about the future going forward. The good news is this, unsolicited five or six of these guys have already said they want to be a part of what we're doing going forward. But right now, these guys need some time off. They really do."

Nearby, Anthony shook his head and mumbled his approval.

Anthony had come a long way. At times, Colangelo had pushed him hard. Now, Colangelo wanted to make sure Anthony didn't get left out. He asked him to speak.

Anthony: "Now that I look back at '04, that experience right there was a blessing to myself, LeBron, Dwyane Wade and also Carlos Boozer. We were at America's lowest point in '04. And to be sitting here in front of you guys tonight and be on top of the world, I think we did a hell of a job putting American basketball back to where it's supposed to be, which is on top of the world."

That sounded like a perfect ending. Except it was time for King James. He opened his mouth, and like an unplugged bathtub, the words came flooding out.

"The game was unbelievable," he said. "I mean, like I said, every possession counted. Every rebound, every pass, every shot, every defensive possession, every offensive possession ...

"We made big plays. We went up nine. Then they came back and hit a three. We hit another three. And they come back and hit two more threes, and then it's a four-point game. And then Kobe hit a four-point play. Then we're up four, and D-Wade gets a wide-open three and puts us up seven. And then they come back and hit a three.

"I'm kind of crazy because I'm watching the game all over again in my head. I'm watching the game all over again. It was at a point where we were about to pull away, and then something happened, and we couldn't pull away.

"The intensity was unbelievable. I think you guys felt the intensity of the game. So if you guys felt it, you know how crazy it was for us."

And right then and there, James decided to end the press conference.

"So, on behalf of us 12 guys, Mr. Colangelo, Coach K, we want to thank you all for being part of 2008."

The players around him were astounded yet again. They all began laughing and hollering, admiring James' gumption.

"Way to wrap it up, baby," Bryant said. "Way to wrap it up."

James was smiling. No one was going to stop him.

No one ever does.

"And we're out of here," he said.

CHAPTER 21

Legacy

....

Bill Russell was living large.

He won a gold medal in1956. He won an NBA championship as a rookie in 1957. He was a black man living in Boston, where the favorite colors were green and white.

Mostly white.

"I was having the time of my life and that's not kidding," Russell said. "The reason I was having the time of my life, first of all, was that (racist fans) gave me something to do in my off time."

More on that later.

"But what I ascribed to do, and did quite well, is every time I came into an adversarial situation, I decided to take control of it so that if a guy came up to me and tried to give me a bad day, I made sure that he was the one who left with the bad day," Russell said. "And so, to do this took thought, planning and discretion and intelligence. That was the way I conducted my life."

Russell won 11 NBA championships in 13 years. He averaged nearly 23 rebounds a game. His battles with Wilt Chamberlain were legendary, the basketball equivalent of Ali-Frazier. You would not go into the lane against the 6-foot-9 Russell, arguably the greatest defensive player in basketball history. And you would not get into his kitchen, either.

"My second year in the league, I bought a house in Reading, Massachusetts," Russell said. "It was a nice little house. And the first time I went on a road trip, my garbage cans were turned over. OK."

Russell surmised that some unfriendly people in the neighborhood were making some kind of statement. The next time Russell's Celtics left for a road trip, it happened again.

"Being the citizen that I am, I wandered down to the police station and talked to the captain of police," Russell said. "I said, 'When I go on the road, my garbage cans get turned over, and I would like to be able to call you guys from the road and have you patrol a little more vigilantly.'

"And he says, 'It's just probably raccoons.' So I said, 'OK, while I'm here, I would like to get a gun permit.' The raccoons heard about that and never turned the trash cans over again. I have never had to buy a gun."

Russell was the first black superstar in the NBA. Throughout his historic, embittered career, he was the cornerstone of the Celtics' dynasty, the guy who set the tone, blocked the shots, set the picks, and cleaned the glass. He and Chamberlain were the only players to ever record 50 or more rebounds in a game.

He later became the first black coach in the NBA, and won his last two titles as player/coach. He was known as the ultimate team guy, and simply the greatest champion in the history of basketball.

"Someone said, 'You won eight straight (championships).' I said, 'Are you kidding?' " Russell said. "It never occurred to us because we always took one year at a time. Last year and next year did not exist for us, so that every championship was an individual team."

What Russell stood for on the basketball court was everything Colangelo had instilled into the Redeem Team. And when the 2009 All-Star Game rolled into Phoenix, it was a time for reunions, parties and new beginnings.

The sport definitely seemed to be functioning on a higher plane, in a better state of harmony. FIBA announced it would alter some of its rules, thus conforming to NBA standards. The trapezoid lane was eliminated, and the three-point arc was moved closer to the American model. Eventually, the rules and dimensions of basketball will be universal:

One world, one game.

Myles Brand, the NCAA president, was diagnosed with pancreatic cancer. But not before he embraced the new regime at USA Basketball, and pledged to work on a new partnership. A year earlier, Brand and Stern unveiled a wide-ranging youth initiative that would stress more education for young players.

This was significant stuff. The three main components of American basketball - the NBA, the NCAA and USA Basketball - were like continents drifting back together.

Meanwhile, the leader of the free world was also a basketball junkie, so much that President Barack Obama publicly desired to bring an indoor court to the White House. Early in his first term, he agreed to form a three-man team from his White House staff and take on Steve Nash, Grant Hill and Shaquille O'Neal.

"We'll probably have Nash on (Obama). USA vs. Canada," Hill joked. "Canada might win this one."

Ah, but what if the new president had filled his cabinet with ringers?

"I'm not too worried about those cats," Nash said.

A few months after co-anchoring the story of Team USA, Bryant and James were developing an unspoken rivalry, lifting the game to rare heights, and the two lit up New York during a special week in February. Bryant established a new Madison Square Garden record with a 61-point performance. Then James came into the building two nights later, and recorded 52 points, 11 rebounds and nine assists.

And just like he did during the Olympics, Wade came roaring back into the conversation. In a span of nine jaw-dropping games, he scored 50, 31, 21, 46, 41, 35, 42, 25 and 48 points. He was carrying the Heat on his shoulders all over again, yet like never before.

The NBA hadn't felt this alive in years.

When the All-Star Game arrived in Phoenix, it was also a bittersweet time for Colangelo. His city had grown up considerably. A new convention center and mass transit system made the weekend a dazzling success. But the Suns were in a stage of deconstruction, and beginning to draw national criticism for bungling a title run, for parting ways with D'Antoni.

In the days leading up to the game, word leaked out that the Suns were about to fire first-year coach Terry Porter. Trade rumors involving O'Neal and Stoudemire filled the air, dominating press conferences. The host organization was blasted for the needless distractions, for interfering with the staged revelry. Colangelo could only wince from the sidelines.

Yet at halftime of the All-Star Game, his moment arrived. Members of the Redeem Team received commemorative rings from Colangelo, who in turn, received a standing ovation from the hometown crowd. He had his name in the rafters. And after all these years, he finally had his championship basketball team.

More telling, six of the star players recommitted to the team for the 2010 FIBA World Championship in Istanbul - Bryant, James, Wade, Chris Bosh, Chris Paul and Dwight Howard. That's a sure sign that things have changed.

"Time will tell, but I believe what we did helped the game of basketball," Colangelo said.

"Those guys over there got it. They got it, and there's no question that they took that experience and brought it back to their respective teams.

"I believe they're better people for what they experienced. They're better basketball players because of what they were exposed to: the games, the staff and the structure. They're more mature. They all grew as leaders. And they brought all of that stuff back to their teams. As a result, I don't think there's any question that the NBA has prospered greatly from what we did in Beijing."

The impact of the Redeem Team is hard to quantify, but impossible to ignore. Like Krzyzewski vowed, the team had played exquisite basketball in Beijing and displayed great dignity. No one thought team members were arrogant, and no one deemed them a bunch of millionaire punks. They changed the way casual fans viewed our Olympic players, and the way our NBA stars viewed playing in the Olympics.

By itself, a gold medal isn't worth a great deal of money. According the Olympic charter, each medal is nearly 93 percent silver. Depending on market prices, the six grams of gold in each medal amount to less than $200. But for the image of the NBA, a league that had been stained by negative stereotypes in the past, those medals were priceless.

"Look, nothing but good can come from what transpired in Beijing because of how it was done," Colangelo said. "It wasn't just the mere accomplishment. It was how we won. We did it with a solid foundation. We did it the right way.

"This was much more than just raising the water level and lifting the boat of USA Basketball. Because of what we did, young kids are aspiring to represent their countries. That makes them better people as they're growing up, long before they go to college. And so what this did was raise the boat for all of basketball."

So it did, and it truly felt like the NBA had turned a significant corner, finally emerging from the post-Jordan fog. A new stable of stars had grown up. Bryant was successfully rehabilitating his damaged reputation. The Celtics and Lakers were relevant once again. And the new sense of brotherhood was most evident after Bryant and O'Neal were chosen to share the All-Star Game's MVP trophy.

Maybe Bryant knew that O'Neal was a fading superstar, unlikely to win any individual awards in the future. Maybe he wanted no part of sharing a trophy with O'Neal. Or maybe it's true that Bryant saw O'Neal's sons ogling the hardware, and told the big guy to keep the trophy all for himself.

Whatever the reason, it was a wonderful gesture. And it was clear Bryant had his eyes on a better trophy, one that was unveiled before the start of the All-Star Game.

When the NBA announced it was renaming its Finals MVP trophy in honor of the legendary Russell, who had recently lost his wife to cancer, the idea seemed momentous. It rewarded the retired center, and all who would win the trophy in the future. The timing was perfect, occurring when the Celtics were reigning champions once again.

It was a cruel twist of irony that Russell had never won the award in his career, and not at all his fault. The NBA didn't introduce the trophy until 1969, the year Russell won his final championship. That year, the MVP award went to a player on the losing team (the Lakers' Jerry West).

"I'm delighted to tell you that we shared (this news) with Marilyn before she died (of cancer), and she didn't tell Bill," Commissioner David Stern said.

Russell was clearly touched by the gesture, and broke down during his press conference.

"It's quite flattering, but I want to explain something to you, all you folks here," Russell said. "This is only the second time I've been out in public since I got my hearing aids. And so when I thought I was going to be with the guys from the press, I put them in the drawer back in my hotel room.

"My wife, Marilyn, used to always ask me why I wouldn't wear my hearing aids, and she bought some fancy hearing aids. And I said, 'The reason I don't wear them is not vanity. The reason I don't wear them is I like what I don't hear.' "

Laughter filled the room.

"But this is one of my proudest moments in basketball because I determined early in my career that the only important statistic in basketball is the final score. And so I dedicated my career to playing, to make sure as often as possible that we were always on the positive side of that final score.

"And like David said, it was ironic that I never won an MVP in the Finals. And it is OK because I will just tell you this: From my second year in the league, I was the most valuable player of the league by the players' votes. But I was second team by the writers' votes."

Russell grinned from ear to ear.

"And that's why I don't wear (the hearing aids)."

Basketball is a breathtaking, breathless game. It is a game that belongs to all of us, available wherever there is a playground, a ball and a rim. But at its highest level, it becomes property of the genetically blessed. It is a sport where men can fly, where one individual can put a franchise on his back. And yet it's the sport where no man can do it alone.

Carmelo Anthony couldn't do it. He endured another tumultuous season, refusing to come out of a regular-season game when benched by Denver coach George Karl. He was suspended one game for insubordination. He rebounded with a terrific post-season, leading the Nuggets to the Western Conference Finals.

LeBron James and Dwyane Wade tried. Neither man had enough supporting cast to make it happen. When James was eliminated in the Eastern Conference Finals, he stormed off the court, refusing to shake hands with the victorious Orlando Magic.

In the end, there was only Kobe, who completed his perfect year with a gold medal and an NBA championship. Two years after demanding a trade from the Lakers, he put his team back on a pedestal. It was the fourth title of his career, and by far the most meaningful.

It was his first without O'Neal, and his push to the finish line was something to behold.

To illustrate his ferocity on the court, he began jutting out his lower jaw and lower teeth after key moments in big games. Teammates likened the look to Hannibal Lecter, and there was no mistaking the intent. In one final snapshot, he engaged in highly physical play with Magic behemoth Dwight Howard, who couldn't believe an Olympic teammate would be so vicious with his elbows.

Just like in China, Bryant wouldn't be denied, and imagine how the ending must've felt. For much his career, he had been stamped as childish, churlish, immature and selfish. He was a coach's nightmare, the kid that Phil Jackson couldn't reach. Now, he was a real leader and an unquestioned champion. He was holding a Finals MVP trophy, the one named after the best team player in history.

For Bryant, the redemption only began in Beijing. It ended in Orlando, where he walked off the court only two titles behind his boyhood idol.

In time, Bryant may yet entrench himself as the second greatest player of all time, surpassing Magic, Oscar, Larry and Wilt in general perception. Or maybe it's Bryant's last stand before James takes over the NBA.

Either way, it's not going to get any easier for the newly crowned. But the game of basketball is sure to get better. No doubt about that.

"I have watched the NBA since 1949, and I knew when I was watching, the players today are just as energetic and just as challenging," Russell said. "The game has evolved. If you say (today's) players don't have good fundamentals, they don't have the fundamentals played back then, but they have the fundamentals to play the game today. I think they are incredible players."

Russell smiled one last time, showing that trademark gap between his front teeth.

"Unfortunately for me, none of them are really good at defense," Russell said.

CHAPTER 22
Bursting the Bubble

R on Thomas claims to have started the first men's salon in Phoenix. He opened the doors to his shop in 1965.

The Suns arrived three years later, and shortly thereafter, a tall, imposing Italian walked into the shop.

It was Jerry Colangelo.

"Those were the days of checkered pants and wide lapels," Thomas said.

For the next 40-plus years, Colangelo would come by every two weeks, even when Thomas moved his shop across town. They developed little quirks, little traditions.

Before every visit, Thomas would have two pieces of Double Bubble gum placed on the barber's chair. Colangelo would come in for his appointment, sit down and have a chew.

"Back in the day, the flavor used to last a long time," Thomas said. "Now, it lasts 15 minutes. He has to chew two pieces of gum during his haircut. Then he goes out the door."

Thomas' first shop had an awning over the front door. When Colangelo would leave, he departed with a signature move. He'd do a hook shot with his bubble gum, launching it on top of the awning.

"One day, I looked up there, and there were about 10 pieces sitting there all hardened," Thomas said. "It got me thinking: If Luis Gonzalez got all that money on eBay for a piece of gum he left on the grass, I wonder what I could get?"

With Colangelo away in Beijing, the barber had a wild idea. He was going to send Colangelo some Double Bubble as a joke. Maybe it would bring him good luck. Certainly, it would make him smile.

Thomas went to a UPS store near his house. He filled out all the requisite forms, including the monetary value of the shipment.

"I put down $10," Thomas said.

And then he spent $88 to send 11 pieces of gum to China.

"The pack had 12, but I broke one off for myself," Thomas said.

According to records, the gum was shipped from Phoenix to Ontario, Canada, to Yinchuan, China, to Beijing. It was examined at every stop. And then the clearing agents in Beijing put a block on the package.

"I go back to UPS and say, 'What about the guarantee?' " Thomas said. "They tell me that once it's overseas, they don't have any control over it. The folks in China might've felt it was some kind of plastic explosive. You know, Double Bubble does have twisted ends."

Thomas is a bit of a character. He's a freelance artist. In 2002, he won the official Ernest Hemingway look-alike contest in Key West, Florida. He once sat on Colangelo's sunglasses, broke them, purchased a replacement pair for $75, and promptly sat on those, too.

"To this day, he still razzes me about that," Thomas said.

But now, Thomas was perplexed. He knew Colangelo always checked into hotels under his own name. He knew Colangelo was staying at the InterContinental Hotel. He checked the phone number twice.

And everywhere they called, they got the same answer.

"They said there was no record of Jerry Colangelo ever being in China," Thomas said. "I mean, we're pretty sure he was there, right?"

The world of basketball would surely bear witness.

BUY A SHARE OF THE FUTURE IN YOUR COMMUNITY

These certificates make great holiday, graduation and birthday gifts that can be personalized with the recipient's name. The cost of one S.H.A.R.E. or one square foot is $54.17. The personalized certificate is suitable for framing and will state the number of shares purchased and the amount of each share, as well as the recipient's name. The home that you participate in "building" will last for many years and will continue to grow in value.

Here is a sample SHARE certificate:

HABITAT FOR HUMANITY

THIS CERTIFIES THAT

YOUR NAME HERE

HAS INVESTED IN A HOME FOR A DESERVING FAMILY

1985-2005

TWENTY YEARS OF BUILDING FUTURES IN OUR COMMUNITY ONE HOME AT A TIME

1200 SQUARE FOOT HOUSE @ $65,000 = $54.17 PER SQUARE FOOT
This certificate represents a tax deductible donation. It has no cash value.

YES, I WOULD LIKE TO HELP!

I support the work that Habitat for Humanity does and I want to be part of the excitement! As a donor, I will receive periodic updates on your construction activities but, more importantly, I know my gift will help a family in our community realize the dream of homeownership. **I would like to SHARE in your efforts against substandard housing in my community!** *(Please print below)*

PLEASE SEND ME _____ SHARES at $54.17 EACH = $ $_____

In Honor Of: _____

Occasion: (Circle One)   HOLIDAY   BIRTHDAY   ANNIVERSARY

　　　　OTHER: _____

Address of Recipient: _____

Gift From: _____   *Donor Address:* _____

Donor Email: _____

I AM ENCLOSING A CHECK FOR $ $_____ PAYABLE TO HABITAT FOR HUMANITY OR PLEASE CHARGE MY VISA OR MASTERCARD *(CIRCLE ONE)*

Card Number _____ Expiration Date: _____

Name as it appears on Credit Card _____ Charge Amount $ _____

Signature _____

Billing Address _____

Telephone # Day _____ Eve _____

PLEASE NOTE: Your contribution is tax-deductible to the fullest extent allowed by law.
Habitat for Humanity • P.O. Box 1443 • Newport News, VA 23601 • 757-596-5553
www.HelpHabitatforHumanity.org

LaVergne, TN USA
25 November 2009
165321LV00002B/2/P